ON THE EDGE

Also by Frances Hunter

A Maverick Elation
Sesame
Mary 'Pickhandle' Fitzgerald

ON THE EDGE

A Woman's Turbulent Life

FRANCES HUNTER

Copyright © 2015 by Frances Hunter

This book includes memoir, memoir-based fiction and poetry. Real events are portrayed to the best of my ability, but memory is notoriously fallible. others may remember events differently. Some names have been changed. Readers should consider the fictional recreation of real events as the works of literature I intend them to be. Some events have been changed for dramatic effect.

ISBN: 978-1-63490-869-6

Library of Congress Control Number: 2015916241

First Edition 2015

For information about permission to reproduce selections from this book contact:

Frances Hunter
Chimera Press
P.O. Box 6700
Santa Fe, NM 87502-2600

Cover design by Todd Engel
Cover photograph: Johannesburg skyline
Printed on acid-free paper

For Brenda Evans

Grateful acknowledgement is made to the following media, in which these memoirs, short stories and poems originally appeared:

"First Aid" read on South African Broadcasting Corporation, 1988;

"Simplicity," "Dust," and "Freedom" in *Sesame: Jo'burg Literary Magazine;*

"Simplicity" in *The Vita Anthology of New South African Fiction,* Justified Press, Johannesburg, 1989 and in *INSIDE AFRICA: A Selection of Stories*, Hodder & Stoughton, Randburg, South Africa, 1992;

"Unrest in Rissik Street" in *Staffrider Magazine*, Vol. 8 No. 1, Ravan Press, Braamfontein, Johannesburg, 1989;

"A Dog's Life" in *Like a House on Fire: Contemporary Women's Writing, Art and Photography from South Africa*, COSAW Publishing, Johannesburg, 1994;

"Something Must Be Done" in *Hippogriff New Writing*, The Hippogriff Press, Johannesburg, 1990;

"Dragons in East Texas" in *Short Story*, University of Texas at Brownsville, Spring 1996;

"On Caddo Lake" in *A Maverick Elation,* Quartz Press, Parkview, Johannesburg, 1999:

"Altar of Air" in *Sin Fronteras/Writers Without Borders, Journal 6*, Las Cruces, New Mexico, 2002;

"A Life Left Behind" in *Looking Back to Place*, Old School Books, Harwood Art Center, Albuquerque, New Mexico, 2008;

"Don't Talk to Strangers" in *Passager*, University of Baltimore, Issue 52, Spring 2012.

For human beings, life is meaningful because it is a story. A story has a sense of a whole, and its arc is determined by the significant moments, the ones where something happens.

—Atul Gawande, Being Mortal

CONTENTS

ENGLAND
1953 – 1956

Don't Talk to Strangers

As far back as I can remember, they've been sticklers for doing the right thing, and I know what the right and proper thing is because they told me, "Children should be seen and not heard." And, "Don't talk with your mouth full." And, "Never make a scene in public." Sometimes, of course, they didn't need to tell me aloud. I heard their intention in my child-soul: *Your behaviour must always be a credit to us.*

Well, what's to be done? Tell them, of course. Imagine: *Mum, Dad, I have something to tell you . . .* then mind going blank.

I simply cannot tell them. I could leave London, go away with no forwarding address and vanish into one of those grey industrial cities to the north where they'd never find me. I could do that. If there was help, I could get a job up there, make a life, new friends. But, wait. They do care. How hard it would be for them never to know what had happened. Think of it: never to know if I'm alive or dead, never to have a body to bury. Cruel.

Hard for me too, whatever I decide, but I can't think about that now.

*

Right now, this room in Notting Hill Gate, half-underground, is my haven, although they wouldn't approve of it. When the sun shines, it bronzes the iron palings topped by trefoil spear-points. The fence keeps drunken pedestrians from toppling into the dank areaway outside my window. The air down here smells of dust, boiled cabbage and mould, almost like the loamy black soil for growing mushrooms. The landlady wouldn't like me to grow mushrooms: not proper behaviour, I know.

My landlady is the only person I've met. We don't talk. I put the rent money under her door upstairs; she puts my rent-book, signed, on the hall-stand just inside the front door. The other lodgers, students mostly, some colonials like me, come and go, always in a hurry. I don't think I've ever been so lonely.

Every morning, I climb grudgingly out of my snug bed and light a match to get the fire going. Shivering, I hold my clothes up to the grate to get some of the damp out of them before getting dressed. Must remember to save shillings for the gas meter. My pajama pants slide up, and my shins turn pink from sitting too close to the fire. Dressed, I go upstairs, take my turn for the bathroom, go downstairs again. The milk in the bottle on my window-sill stays cool and fresh. After cornflakes and tea, I go out and walk the streets, searching.

The red sanctuary light glows in Brompton Oratory. I used to walk past it every day before I gave up my job. I need to talk to someone; I need someone to advise me, but when I'm tempted to go in there, the image of a man in a black cassock comes to me, as forbidding as the façade of that building. I know what he would say.

Every day I walk to find my answer, walk these grimy streets, buildings besmirched by the industrial revolution, walk past craters, charred bomb sites, where homes once were. I wish I wasn't doing this. Although I'm walking, I'm still dithering.

Once, while I waited to cross a road, a man standing on the platform of a bus going slowly past called out to me, "Cheer up, ducks. It can't be that bad."

It is that bad, I wanted to say to him. Of course, I didn't, but the rest of that day and the days since then I remember him—an ordinary, slightly shabby man—and every time I think of him it's like the way—after a long hard winter—the first daffodils of spring lift your heart, and I wish I was the kind of girl who would rush up to the bus, jump on the platform and hug him in gratitude. Girls like me don't talk to strangers, never mind hug them.

Some days, rain pelts down, buckets down in the proverbial cats and dogs. I sometimes shelter briefly under a narrow parapet, then run and stand under an awning over a restaurant or hotel entrance, stand there as if waiting for someone to join me. After a while the doorman gives me dirty looks. When he's about to beckon a policeman, I give up and come back home. I light the gas in the fireplace, undress, dry myself, put on my flannel pajamas and hold my sodden clothes up to the blue flames to dry them for tomorrow.

Back in bed to keep warm while saving gas, eyes closed, I see myself on the screen of my eyelids back in the reference room of the North Kensington Library, see myself reading the words in the Encyclopaedia Britannica: five years of prison for me, eight years for him or her. I didn't know it was such a crime.

The risk! Do the other patrons innocently reading about what to plant in spring . . . do they hear my heart thumping in its cage of ribs, my heart trying to escape as I, myself, want to escape?

I can't confide in anyone, but that's not the only risk. I could even die. No. Can't think like that. But I can't look for another job until . . . In the evenings, I heat tomato soup from a can on the gas ring and toast a slice of bread at the grate to go with it.

Some days, the sky looks rosy through the iron fence when I wake: I'm late, so I leap out of bed, quickly make tea and toast.

I walk south from Notting Hill Gate, down to Church Street, and cross Kensington High Street. Usually I turn west, then south again on Earls Court Road, Finborough, and Gunter Grove. After that, sometimes I take New Kent Road, sometimes Wandsworth. Each day I take a bus to the point I left off walking the day before. Wandsworth Bridge lies ahead; I won't cross it; Battersea on the other side doesn't look promising.

There are a few days when the sun stays out, and I walk all day, walk with hope that I will track down my quarry, but darkness falls and with it my hopes for that day.

Some mornings, while I'm putting on my coat to go out, the rain starts again, and not just a gentle drizzle. I get back into bed and huddle, head under the covers, all thought of walking gone, all thought in abeyance.

Sometimes, I confess, when the rain gets to me, I duck into a Lyon's Corner House. Although I have to conserve my savings, I pay for a cup of tea at the counter and stir a teaspoon of sugar into it. The teaspoon is attached by a chain to the counter, which must be a leftover custom from war-time and sugar rationing, seven years ago. Surrounded by the smell of damp woollen overcoats and the murmur of voices, I cup my hands around the heavy white ceramic cup to warm them.

If I don't succeed soon, the end of the week will be here. Another week gone by. I'm running out of time, and I'm getting more queasy and tired every day. My money is almost gone too. The king, George VI, died today, 6th February 1952—it's on all the newspaper placards—and the country is in mourning. Princess Elizabeth will be queen. Funny that I'm almost the same age as her little sister Margaret Rose.

What keeps me going is thinking of the doctor I had hoped would help. I made the appointment with his receptionist, saying I wasn't sick, I was new to the area and needed to speak to him about getting on his panel of patients. After a long time in the chilly waiting-room with people sniffing and coughing, I sat on the other side of his wide desk. He was affable, plump and pink, able to afford expensive restaurants, eat caviar. When he heard what I wanted, how his face changed! He rose from his chair, mouth opening and closing like a goldfish.

"Get out! Get out before I call the police."

Well, I'm not stupid: I know when a cause is hopeless. And I don't make scenes. I did get out with my head held high so the whole waiting room wouldn't know how I felt. At least, he didn't trick me into waiting until the police arrived.

Outside, at the bus stop, I thought about what to do next. The asphalt of the roadway was still dark from the night's rain. A middle aged man came to sit at the other end of the bench. From the paper bag he carried, he took out a two-inch heel of a bread loaf. He broke it and tossed crumbs to the pigeons. They seemed to know him and had assembled.

"Take this and eat," he said aloud to the grey and shimmering congregation at his feet. "Increase and multiply."

You wouldn't think London was already chock-full of pigeons, bird-shit whitening the head and shoulders of all the statues.

I sometimes wonder if I imagined this man. Who knows? There are odd people in every city.

The next best bet would be a chemist—similar to doctors but since that pink and shining doctor's threat, I bypass any number of Boot's chemist shops, sparkling with cleanliness and rectitude, too dangerous to try.

I walk down the stairs into the underground, push through the turnstile, knowing I'm going into its maze of tunnels and rails below the frantic city, into the mixture of smells, coal dust, oil, the hot steel of the rails, cigarette smoke, unwashed humanity.

I am not going anywhere on the Tube train. I have simply come down here to be among people with a purpose, people who know where they are going and why, hoping it will brush off on me. I stand on a platform at Eaton Square station. People embark and disembark. Very orderly they are, British people, but it becomes too much: all the endless tributaries and distributaries of people coming and going about their business, not one of them seeing me as a person. This is what being in an ant colony underground would be like.

I go into the Ladies, push a penny into the brass box at the door of a cubicle. With my penny I am buying time to be alone. I sit on the lid of a toilet and read the writing on the walls. Enclosed in a heart, "JB loves LM" "Shirley Kent is a tart" "I want you Cedric please call."

What would I write? Is there a way to express in words an anguished scream? No.

It will have to be enough to know that there are other people with something to say that they will not say aloud and that we try to leave our secrets in the underworld.

I think the die was cast after my true love said to me, "No, it's impossible, I have to finish my studies, I can't marry until I can afford to support a wife." Very proper: that's probably what he learned from *his* parents. Never mind that I came as a stranger to this country because he begged me to. Never mind that we once made our own springtime. A chunk of flesh torn from my chest. Hearts may mend, but mending trust is something else. It'll soon be Valentine's Day, patron saint of lovers. What a joke!

†

I walk farther than usual—not raining for a change—and get into a rundown part of town. I'd soon be in the slums by the look of it. I stroll three times past a seedy apothecary. The man standing behind the counter—must be the owner, a chemist—catches my eye the first time and seems to be waiting for each of my reappearances. He is the one. I cross to the other side of the road and linger in the doorway of a fish and chip shop, where I can watch his store-front. His assistant, a youngish woman, leaves. It must be closing time. She trots off on her high heels clickety-click down to the bus stop. I wait until the bus she enters whisks her off and around the next corner, out of sight. It is time.

I re-cross the road, stand outside the plate glass and look at him steadily through the large dusty bottles of red and green liquid on the shelf just inside, his window dressing. He returns my look with a long gaze of his own. He is waiting for me. We have never seen each other before, but we two, predator and prey, recognise our own. Which the predator? Which the prey?

He opens the door. "Why have you come?"

"I need your help."

"Who told you to come to me?"

"No one told me."

"Then why? Why me?"

"I saw your eyes . . . and you have a kind face."

He gives me a wondering, distrustful look. He may turn me away. An ocean of time passes while I can only wait.

"Kind? Me?" he says finally. I see that, despite himself, he is moved. I did see kindness in his face, but it may be that no one has ever called him kind before. He will do what I ask.

"It will cost fifty pounds."

"I don't have that much."

"What do you have?"

"Eight pounds." I wait briefly while he considers. He mustn't refuse. "I'll pay the whole amount after I get a job. Next week, I hope."

He goes to the entrance and carefully locks the door, then turns off the main light while I stand waiting.

"We won't talk about money. Come." He leads the way into a small cluttered back room, a sort of cloakroom. He motions to a rack where his overcoat is hanging. I hang mine next to his.

"I have a problem sometimes," he says. He puts his arms around me and I see his sallow disappointed face clearly. His teeth are crooked. He is quite old, in his thirties.

"With your wife?"

A tiny pause, then he nods. So not only with his wife.

"I've always been faithful to my fiancé," I tell him.

He understands what I mean. "We needn't," he says, "you know."

"All right."

He has his usual problem with me. Why did he expect it to be different? Finally he stops trying, sighs deeply and rearranges his clothing. I understand that he knows it is not my fault. We wrap our arms around each other, hold one another. We stand like this for a long time—I don't know how long—I lose track of time. I am aware of us only as two broken anonymous people comforting each other. Perhaps being one half of an old married couple feels like this.

He gently lets go of me, and we stand again as separate people.

"Your fiancé," he says, "he won't marry you?"

"He broke off the engagement when I told him."

"All right," he says. "This is the arrangement. I will do what you ask. For your part, you will swear to tell no one it was me. If you do, it will destroy me. Do you understand that?"

I see fear in his eyes. "I understand. I would never tell."

He decides he can trust me.

"And the next thing. If anything goes wrong—although I don't believe anything will, nothing ever has—you must promise to call an ambulance. I'm serious."

He is deadly serious, and I see that I am putting my future in his hands. I will trust him with my life.

*

I wait for him now. It will be done. While I wait, I think of peaches. It's a long time since I've eaten a peach, eaten any fruit. Now in my grey time, I think salvation may lie in remembering the peaches of summer, the soft, sinful, succulent, self-indulgence of peaches, peaches that memorialise new mornings and the soft fuzzy-headed infant I will never see and will mourn. I am trying to remember the song of peaches, peaches singing their sonata through blossom, bud and fruit time. I am trying to remember the smell of peaches, the never-bottled, impossible to mimic, innocence aroma of the lust of peaches. I want to hold on to everything peaches have to say.

NORTHERN RHODESIA
1956 – 1968

Ndola and Mufulira

Northern Rhodesia. What did we, the naïve young newly-married couple, know about the country? Only that it was a British colony north of Southern Rhodesia, which in turn was just north of South Africa, Ken's birthplace and home.

We did not want to remain in the cold and fog and damp of England, where he had recently passed his law exams and qualified as a barrister and solicitor and where we had recently married. I was twenty-five years old, saved in the nick of time from being an old maid.

He had chosen to study English law because he did not want to take Latin as one of his subjects. It turned out to be a foolish choice, partly because Roman Dutch law, requiring Latin, was the legal system in South Africa, so he would not be able to practice law in his home country. Also, the sun was setting on countries in the British Empire, where he could practice English law. A few British colonies, such as Hong Kong, remained in existence. He replied to advertisements in several. A law firm in Ndola, Northern Rhodesia, offered him a position.

We left London by small twin-engine plane and hopped to refuel, stay-over and sight-see in Malta and in Mersa Matruh on the Mediterranean in Egypt and somewhere on the Nile and onward. By then I was too weary to remember the next stop or stops on our way. And so we arrived in Ndola, our worldly possessions, including wedding presents, in four suitcases. To avoid our luggage being overweight and having to pay a penalty, I carried the electric iron in my fashionably-shaped bucket-bag. Even in tropical Africa, I would wash and iron Ken's white shirts and wash, starch and iron the white winged-collars that attached to them, and he would wear the traditional barrister's wig and black gown in a courtroom where a ceiling fan was the "air conditioner" of that time and place.

We found the law firm—the only one in town—to be a one-storey whitewashed building with a verandah fronting the unpaved main street, and we rented a small house, also whitewashed with a corrugated iron roof, not far away. I learned the meaning of "red dust of Africa" intimately when light breezes carried that powdery dust into every cranny of our new home, into every corner of every drawer, and into the seams of our clothing. I was daunted by the wood-fired stove in the ninety degree kitchen but would not be mastered by it. I was entranced by the large romantic and aromatic moonflower bush in front of the house until told that it was the poisonous datura plant.

Len Catchpole was the mayor of Ndola. His usual business was town auctioneer; his sideline was coffin-making. At the auction I attended, where I hoped to buy essential furniture, he opened the door of a wardrobe, peered inside for a while and then, to my astonishment, informed the prospective bidders, "Inside this piece of furniture is a turd of human origin."

Ken was one of the four lawyers in Richmond Smith's offices, and I joined the firm as a legal typist to type wills, conveyances of property, and letters, both accusatory and defensive, until the bulge of my pregnancy at eight months forced me to sit too far away from the typewriter.

One of other lawyers was Fintan Burke, an Irishman. It was well known that when he'd taken a drink too many his wife Bunty chased him out of the house with a broom.

Our neighbour across the road, superintendent of the prison at Bwana Mkubwa, was convicted of stealing prison blankets for profit and left home to spend time in his own prison, the only white inmate. His dog, a bull terrier, was also anti-social: he picked fights with the dog we acquired, a boxer, and redesigned his features.

The months continued dry with increasing heat into the so-called "suicide month" of October. In November, the long-awaited rains came and flying ants swarmed, to the delight of laughing brown-skinned youngsters who pulled off their wings and crammed the ant-torsos into their mouths.

After my first child, my son Alan, was born in February 1958, I learned about the flies that laid their eggs in the toweling diapers hung in the sun to dry. The eggs hatched in the urine-damp diapers on the baby, and the maggots burrowed into his tender flesh.

"I thought everyone knew about *putzi* flies," said Dr. Sinclair.

That was the second black mark against him, the first being that he had been too lazy to turn up for the birth in the cottage hospital in the early hours of the morning when the nurse delivered my first born. Nevertheless, he billed for and was paid for the delivery.

I followed his instructions about *putzi* eggs; they could be destroyed by carefully ironing every inch of the line-dried diapers, which added to my ironing chore. I followed his instructions about the *putzi* maggots. When it was time, I covered the first angry red burrow on the baby's buttocks with Vaseline and watched. As soon as the worm's head emerged to take a breath of air, I squeezed the whole thing out and popped it into a jar. I collected the larva in the jar, and they metamorphosed into flies before we left Ndola. I was glad to have the opportunity of presenting the buzzing jar to the doctor as a memento of our fleeting time together.

Ken gained experience in Richmond Smith's law firm, and about two years after our arrival he opened a law practice in Mufulira, a copper-mining town not far away, where we would spend another ten years in Northern Rhodesia.

Ken joined the Rotary Club in Mufulira, and I learned that it was a charitable organisation for professional men that did good works and that I was an adjunct, a Rotary Ann: women's liberation had not yet arrived. Ken and I once drove miles into the bush with camping gear and three small children. Rotary supplied drilling equipment, and the men struck water and drilled a well for villagers of the Bemba tribe, whose women previously had to walk a couple of miles carrying buckets of water from the Kafue River to their huts.

In Mufulira, my days were spent at home, first in John Roberts Road, when Alan and Jocelyn were very young, and then in Bell Avenue, a short cul-de-sac facing the Convent School in its large grounds, where Alan, Jocelyn and Barbara started school. I could watch them walk down our driveway, across the road and onward toward the classrooms. The nuns were strict but kind, Alan remembers. He quickly learned to read and his teacher let him read books from the school library in addition to the "Janet and John" first readers he found boring. The nuns also allowed him to collect eggs from their battery hens and to befriend Shaka and Dingaan, their German shepherd guard dogs. Jocelyn, the big sister, kept an eye out for Barbara and stood up for her when she was once falsely accused of some petty offence.

My days were occupied with cooking, sewing the children's clothes and my own, reading, refurbishing the house by painting the walls and tiling floors, creating and tending a rose garden, typing a recipe book for a church sale, and playing Scrabble with my friend Betty Mills. She had daughters the same age as mine, and they became friends, while Alan's good friend was Gordon McConville, who lived almost next door. One of my favourite memories is of time spent with the children while they splashed and cooled themselves in a canvas pool set up in the front garden. Looking back, I remember those years as a halcyon interlude.

The spell was broken when Ken insisted on sending Alan to boarding school: "He should not be tied to his mother's apron strings." Ken wanted to send him at age seven, far too young to leave home. Also, Alan was sensitive and not good at sports, which did not bode well for him in a school based on the English public school model. By pleading I gained a year, and Alan went at age eight to Eagle School in Southern Rhodesia (later Zimbabwe). He had previously done very well in his studies, but at Eagle the results on his report cards were erratic, he had no friends, and he was miserable for three years. His bipolar symptoms may have first shown themselves at this time.

Northern Rhodesia gained independence from Britain in 1964 and was renamed Zambia

In 1968 Ken and I with three of our children drove in two cars from Mufulira to Johannesburg, South Africa. Alan was left at Eagle School to rejoin us at the beginning of his next school holidays and to be sent as a boarder to St. John's College in Johannesburg.

We drove for the last time through Zambia's parched, flat land dotted with stunted trees and house-high anthills. Dust devils twirled, and on the roads mirages ahead beckoned. Strip-roads required intense concentration to keep all four wheels on the two narrow concrete strips. When another car approached, we passed each other by driving with only two wheels on one of the strips.

The price of copper fell not long after we left and the economy collapsed. The country would never be the same.

Cottage Hospital

He had returned from the law offices after the day's work. They sat in the living room of the small house while he sipped a frothy-headed Castle lager from the antique pewter mug she had given him.

"I think we should go now," she said.

He said with complete conviction, "It's too soon."

It was February 17, 1958. Her small case was packed with toiletries and light reading matter, enough for a week's stay in the cottage hospital. She had read and reread *Childbirth Without Fear* by Dr. Grantley Dick-Reid and had practiced the breathing exercises.

"No. Now! We need to go now."

He frowned. A small breeze wafted through the burglar bars of the open windows, heralding a cooler night temperature.

"It's not that far," he said. "We can be there in no time."

"I know, but I'll feel better if we go now." After a pause she added, knowing it would convince him, "You wouldn't want to deliver it in the car."

He stood abruptly, went to the bedroom and returned with her case. In the cream-coloured VW Beetle they drove without speaking. It was a small town, and the red corrugated iron roofs of the cottage hospital soon came in sight. When she stepped onto the gravel of the parking area in the tropical heat, a sudden chill filled her body. She stumbled but quickly righted herself.

He came round to her side of the car. She leaned against the solid strength of him, looked into his face and said, "I'm afraid."

"It'll be all right," he said. He was trying to be kind. She threw her arms around him, around the strong trunk of him, clinging, wanting to believe he was right.

He loosened her arms. "We can't stand here."

They walked toward the one-storey yellow brick building. The entryway led to an open square courtyard. Covered walkways around the courtyard sheltered doors. A few open doors revealed two-bed wards. They entered the office on the right of the entryway, where she signed in.

"We'll let the doctor know," the nurse said and led them to a ward, where the other bed was empty. She was handed a white cotton gown.

"I'll leave you now," the nurse said.

"I'll be off too," he said.

"Please won't you stay?"

"I have to work tomorrow and need my sleep. I'll come and see you early in the morning."

She wouldn't plead.

She walked to the door, closed it, undressed and folded her clothes neatly on the chair next to her bed. She lay on the bed, looked up at the ceiling and saw herself like a crusader's statue on his tomb. But a crusader would not have the discomfort of a huge belly, making it impossible to lie comfortably on his back.

She heaved herself off the bed and tried not to waddle along the walkway to the toilet. There, something besides urine emerged from her body, something odd. Could it be the cord? Felt more like a tiny hand. Then it was gone, almost as if she had imagined it.

"Sister!" she called on the way back.

"What is it?"

"I felt something come down."

"Greta!" the nurse shouted. Then two of them, one on each side, holding her arms, were walking her stumbling to the delivery room. A woman in one of the wards screamed. Greta said, "The louder the screams, the bigger the gift from the husband." The first one snickered. They were talking about couples, quite unlike Ken and herself, but, whatever happened, she would not scream. The nurses increased their pace, almost dragging her to a doorway in the far corner of the courtyard.

They settled her in the high bed with white enameled bars at its head. "It'll be a while," the first nurse said, "Try to rest."

Time slowed in the cheerless white room, where she lay on her side with a white sheet draped over her. The pain came and went, constantly surging and retreating, like waves at a beach. When it swept over her, all thoughts went into limbo. When the wave ebbed, her mind returned to her and she returned to herself.

The high window was on the leeward side of the hospital. No breeze stirred the heavy white cotton curtain. Outside, the birds were silent; they would have tucked their heads comfortably under their wings. Her own head was making the pillow damp.

When the next wave came, she tried to escape it by imagining that she was a bird and could soar out of the window. No use. It had to be endured while it lasted.

After that wave, she did succeed in seeing herself flying. She flew to where the trumpet-shaped moonflower gleamed ghostly white in front of their small house with its tiny second bedroom waiting for the child. She would not go inside, where he could be sleeping.

The tide came in faster, receded more slowly.

The author of *Childbirth Without Fear* had lied. Dr. Grantley Dick-Reid said fear caused the pain. Women in primitive parts of the world, who toiled in the fields and were not afraid gave birth in a furrow, slung their infants on their backs and continued toiling. He would say the pain was her fault because she allowed herself to fear. But hadn't the pain had come before the fear?

Surely, the waves were closer together.

If he were here, he could tell the nurses when it was time to call the doctor. But he might not because both of his parents were doctors, and he believed that doctors should not be called at night; they needed their rest.

The intensity of the pain left her exhausted.

If he were here, she would not be alone in the sleeping world, alone and lonely beyond measure. They would have let him stay until it was time for the baby to be born. They were short-handed and would have been glad of his help. Would this night be a turning point, between before and after, between him and her?

When a spasm of pain was upon her, there was no return to ordinary thought. There was no past or future. The world was only the present time that had to be endured until she was released. Her body was in the grip of a foreign force, a conquering army that could do as it would; it was no longer her own.

The times of release grew shorter. Pain became continuous like time. It filled her completely and dulled her mind. Her world was that pain. She lay stupefied.

A cock crowed in the distance. She roused herself to turn to look at the tray on a stand near the bed. On the tray a small white cloth half-covered shining stainless steel instruments. They must have forgotten her. If they knew how she felt, they would not have left a scalpel so near her hand.

The day was starting to brighten the white curtain when an older nurse came in, probably on the day shift. The nurse said with an Irish lilt, "I'll examine you, if you don't mind."

She watched the nurse and saw the light go out of the cheerful face that then loomed large, close to her, and spoke distinctly. "I want you to hold on now. Just trust me."

There was nothing she could do but trust. She gripped the white enameled iron bars at the head of the bed and pulled hard, pulled her head through the bars for an eternity, and then it was ended.

The baby breathed but did not cry. Wrapped in white flannelette on a stand nearby, it was pale, angelic-looking.

"You have a son," the nurse said. "Your guardian angel was watching over you. He was sideways, couldn't be born. You'd both have died if I hadn't turned the child."

She looked up and saw her husband standing behind the nurse.

The Sanity of Bread

Oh, how I hated those formal dinners, but this one was nearly over. The black waiters, white clad and wearing white gloves, were serving Peach Melba and filling glasses again, this time with a dessert wine, a sweet marsala. Despite the large wooden fan turning overhead, the faces of the club members had turned a deeper shade of pink, not just from wearing dinner jackets and starched shirts in the tropical heat. More than a little tipsy, they had begun the end-of-evening traditional bantering across the tables arranged in a large rectangle and covered with white damask linen.

Seated with their wives, many of the successful men of the copper mining town in Northern Rhodesia were gathered together: from the mayor to the owners of the general store and pharmacy to one of the only two doctors. Ken was the town's only lawyer. He sat on my right with his black-clad back turned to me while he undertook a rather long obligatory chat with the attractive woman on his right. I went to these Ladies' Night dinners with bad grace. I begrudged being considered an accessory, and being called a Rotary Ann always made me think of myself as a Raggedy Ann doll spinning with woolly blonde braids horizontal. But a good wife could not refuse to attend.

The distinguished looking man now seated on my left had arrived late and had been introduced as a visiting Rotarian. He was silver-haired with a lined face and deep-set eyes under heavy brows. He looked interesting, intriguing even, and my romantic imagination told me he had hidden depths. But, alas, he was engaged in conversation with the talkative, vivacious woman on his left. My task—between standing for the anthem, toasting the queen's health and listening to speeches—had been to appear to be enjoying myself while silently picking at the shrimp cocktail followed by the roast beef and Yorkshire pudding I would normally have enjoyed.

Whose idea was it to arrange diners two by two, as if preparing to board Noah's ark? I was dressed in my stilettos and a silvery dress with black velvet shoulder straps that hugged my figure, appropriate for a consort.

The latecomer on my left finally turned to me. "Excuse me," he said, "I've been speaking with my major business contact. It's the first opportunity I've had and probably the last."

"Speaking of the last," I said, "the last time I was at one of these dinners, I sat next to the town's only eligible bachelor. He was renowned for being able to pay flattering compliments to even the plainest woman."

"And how did he compliment you?"

"He told me I had the cleanest ears he had ever seen."

My dinner companion threw back his head and laughed.

"What brings you to the Copperbelt?" I asked. "It's not exactly a tourist destination."

"You've heard of the Yad Vashem in Israel, I'm sure. I'm touring to promote adding something to the museum to commemorate gentiles who . . ."

Just then, I was distracted by a bread roll flying across the open space between the tables. It would have been flung by Ken. Like the childish bantering, it was probably an expression of unacknowledged rivalry. Another bread roll appeared and whizzed past my companion's head, and before long the air was full of these playful missiles.

The man beside me pushed his chair back slightly with an air of disengaging himself and leaving the scene. He was about to speak, and I leaned closer to hear. "You don't throw bread," he said softly, as though to himself. "Anything else you can throw, but you don't throw bread." He stood and walked to the back of the room, where I joined him.

He must have endured hunger, I thought. Could he have been in the war? Be a concentration camp victim? It seemed impolite to ask. I took a chance and said, "I think bread is important in your rituals and mine."

"The reason for its sacredness," he answered slowly, "is the toil in its ordered sowing. Think of the slow growing and gathering in season, the careful grinding and sifting, and the patient kneading and leaving to rise. And the putting into ovens."

That last phrase chilled me, that phrase together with his eastern European accent. Did it mean what I suspected? It would be crude to ask. I remembered a poem I had written about bread and quoted part of it: "And the sowing maleness and incubating femaleness of bread and of the warm undeniably good smell of its birthing."

"That's lovely," he said, and then said seriously, taking my hand, "You and I will remember this evening and each other."

Bread rolls were still flying across the tables. "Yes," I agreed. "I will remember, and tonight I've learned that when the world seems mad there is always the sanity of bread to hold on to."

"I leave for Johannesburg tomorrow," he said. "So this is goodbye." He kissed my cheek like a familiar uncle and opened the heavy wooden double doors and went out.

I waited at the back of the room for Ken, always the last to leave a party, and wondered about my new acquaintance. Were numbers tattooed on his arm under the white shirt with the glittering gold cufflink? It did not matter. What mattered was that he would never throw bread and he would know when it was the right time to leave a party or anything else he was engaged in. And it mattered that we had made poetry together. That was something to remember.

A Life Left Behind
—Zambia 1956 to 1968

It was being present, but not part of it,
wanting to believe home was somewhere else.
It was stupefying heat, late annual rains,
the first rain like hailstones, tin roof
creaking in protest, fly screens
on windows, fruit bats flying in and out
of eaves morning and evening,

It was anthills high as the house, millions
of ants, blue-headed lizards, black crows
in white vests, and small gray ant-lions
in the sand, waiting in their holes for ants
to fall in. It was copper mines where black-
skinned workers in thousands went down
holes and dug out wealth for whites.

It was our four children, born in Ndola
and Kitwe. It was the other family at the end
of the yard, wife sitting on their doorstep
all day, husband, son of a chief, sweeping
our floors, calling us Bwana and Dona,
drinking milk straight from the bottle
when our backs were turned.

It was flame trees and kingfishers.
It was gymkhanas, it was polo, it was
the Mine Club, its cinema—The Sound
of Music—its library—Monserrat
and Mickey Spillane; it was going with
Rotary Club and Rotary Anns into the bush
to create a water supply for villagers.

It was hostility in the eyes of youths
on sidewalks, youths walking five abreast
on sidewalks; it was parents prosecuted
because their toddler scribbled over
the newspaper photo of the President. It was
dust devils whirling down dirt roads
like anger incarnate. It was murder.

It was drumbeats in the night, morse-coding
"Get Out!" It was packing urgently, driving
to exile, forgetting the child's doll in the tree
house, but taking guilt and fear. Afterwards,
it was copper price falling, breeding stock
slaughtered for meat, corruption, famine, AIDS,
and seeing the disaster, far from home.

SOUTH AFRICA
1968 – 1994

Bird!

I was studying for my BA in social work at the University of South Africa (UNISA), the government's distance learning university. As a married woman, I had no money of my own, but when my father left me a bequest I spent it on university fees. I had been allowed by the university to enroll on the grounds of "mature age" since I was over twenty-five, well over that age, actually. My final high school year Cambridge Entrance examination, in which I had achieved good marks, was not acceptable for enrollment because my subjects had not included Afrikaans.

Now in my final year with UNISA, I would be working with two clients from welfare organisations for the casework practice requirement. I already had one client—through the Mental Health Society—a man with schizophrenia. For the other, the Children's Hospital suggested a mother with a five-year-old child who had a psychological problem and a husband who appeared to have rejected the child. That would broaden my experience.

I telephoned Helen Fisher. "The Children's Hospital said you called about your child. I'm in my final year of social work studies. May I come and see you?"

I drove south into a suburb of small working class houses. At the door, Helen, pale with dark hair and dark rings under her eyes, motioned me into the sitting room, where we stood and I said, "Would you like to tell me about your little girl?"

"Come and see Amanda. She's having her lessons with me."

We left the sitting room—cheap mass-produced lounge suite, no bookcase, no television—to the dining room, where Amanda sat at the table. She was healthy-looking, chubby with rosy cheeks, dark hair like her mother's, and eyes a deep clear blue under well-defined eyebrows.

"What a lovely child!"

"The clinic nurse said maybe she should go to a place like the Hamlet to get training, but she knows her letters, so she could go to school and learn to read. Show the lady, Amanda. What's this?"

"A," said Amanda without looking at me.

"Good girl." Amanda did not smile. "And what's this?"

"F"

"Very good. And this?"

"E"

"No, Amanda. No!" Amanda's expression did not change.

I said, "She did get some right, and look how similar E and K are. It's easy for a child to mix them up."

"She got K right yesterday. It's taking a while." Helen sighed then brightened. "I taught her to set the table. Set the table for me, Amanda."

Amanda went to the drawer in the sideboard, took out two knives and forks and placed them correctly on the table in front of two of the chairs.

Helen smiled "See, she can learn."

"I see that."

*

I visited Helen once a week and soon gained the impression that she looked forward to my visits as opportunities to talk and to show off Amanda's progress. Amanda remembered more letters of the alphabet but, strangely, did not seem to recognise me.

On trips to the park with its children's playground, Helen told me that Amanda had been rough with the other children, who had gone crying and complaining to their mothers, "She hit me. She pushed me." The mothers did not greet her the next time she went to the park, so she stopped going.

At the grocery store, Helen saw the looks that other shoppers gave the little girl and put off that outing for as long as she could.

She had taken Amanda for check-ups at the clinic, keeping all her appointments. The clinic sister had said the child was slow to crawl and to walk and had given Helen exercises for her, which she performed religiously, and Amanda had progressed. But ever since the clinic sister had said she should send Amanda for training, Helen had not gone back.

She and her child had become more and more isolated, and Amanda was a demanding child. Helen had no friends, and I believed that I could provide some of the emotional support she lacked by being an interested listener who understood what she was enduring.

*

During the year I presented weekly reports to my supervisor, Jean Stewart. I was lucky to have as my mentor one of the most experienced and respected social workers in the city, and she, like me, was interested in psychodynamics. We came to agree that Helen was depressed and had good reason to be. About the child, we were not so sure. Amanda did not look at me directly, did not make eye contact, did not smile, repeated words, repeated body movements, had tantrums and could be aggressive. All of those behaviours could be symptoms of retardation or of autism. Autism was certainly a possibility because Amanda could learn. If the child had potential that could be developed, she should have that opportunity. It needed to be checked out.

I told Helen, "You could have her tested."

"What kind of tests?"

"Educational tests, psychological tests at the Children's Hospital. If they find she's autistic, she might have treatment. And there's a school for autistic children."

"The clinic nurse told me to have her tested, but she didn't say anything about treatment and the school."

Encouraged, Helen spent more time with Amanda in the three weeks before the appointment, evenings as well as day-time hours, and in addition to lessons with the alphabet she taught Amanda numbers, plastic numbers in primary colours.

I had given the psychiatrist at the Children's Hospital, Dr. Carol Wallace, copies of my weekly reports to Jean Stewart. The last report set out the grounds for considering autism, which Jean had approved. Now Dr. Wallace wanted to see me. I arrived promptly for my appointment with her, but time went by while I waited in the office: quarter past, twenty past, twenty-five past. Would she deliberately fail to show up? She must have forgotten or been detained elsewhere. What on earth did she want to see me about?

With my ears alert for the sound of footsteps approaching and my heart a drum-beat tattoo in my ribs, I went to the filing cabinet, opened the drawer labeled "Students," pulled out my file and quickly scanned the last report. A red *X* was scratched across my section titled "Assessment." In the margin, words in red shouted *Rubbish!* And *Outrageous!* And *Who does she think she is!* At the foot of the page, my report was graded *D.*

A sudden chill seized me; I shoved the file back, slammed the drawer shut and left the office. It wasn't fair. Dr. Wallace was a Behaviorist, saw people in terms of stimulus and response, like Pavlov and his salivating dog. That could be the reason. But in case conferences, psychologists and psychology students presented assessments and tentative diagnoses, similar to mine. Did Dr. Wallace view social work as an inferior qualification, the way some psychologists did out of professional jealousy? Many students did not like her. Whatever her reasons, she could cause me to fail my final exam. The practical work counted for half the marks.

*

On the day of Amanda's appointment for tests at the Children's Hospital, I stood outside the front door and watched Helen pull Amanda by the hand up the short incline from the bus stop.

"She's been irritable and difficult since she woke up."

"Could be because she knows you're anxious."

With Amanda settled between us, we sat in the waiting-room.

A nurse introduced herself. "I'll take the little girl for her tests."

Never before having left her mother, Amanda pulled back and whined, "No. No."

The nurse picked her up, kicking and crying, and carried her through a doorway out of the waiting room. Helen and I waited again in silence. Helen, with eyes closed, clasped her hands together, while I hoped hard for a diagnosis of autism for Helen's sake.

In a short while, Dr. Wallace, in a white coat, came to the door and beckoned me. How could they have completed the tests so soon?

"How dare you waste our time like this? The child is ineducable."

Dr. Wallace ushered me back to the waiting room, where she smiled at Helen and said, "I'm sorry, dear. I can't tell you anything. We couldn't test her."

We walked out of the hospital together in silence, Helen dragging the child roughly while I remained stunned by Dr. Wallace's quick diagnosis of "ineducable." Outside the entrance, I said to Helen, "You must be very disappointed. I'm so sorry."

Helen did not reply. I was sorry I had given her false hope and sorry for the child and sorry for myself.

Rain fell in a cold drizzle. I walked with Helen to the bus shelter. Amanda whined and pulled at her mother's sleeve. Helen's arm swung round, and her fingers left welts on the child's cheek.

I said, "It's okay to be angry, Helen, but it's not Amanda's fault. Maybe it's no one's fault."

*

The next time I saw Helen, she told me that she had telephoned Child Welfare for a list of Children's Homes. They had asked her to come in to talk about a placement for her child, but she insisted on having the list first. With Amanda, day after day she took buses to the Homes on the list that looked possible.

"I know you're full," she said at each one, "but I want her name on the waiting list."

She had given up lessons with Amanda, she told me, and whenever waiting for a vacancy became so unbearable that she thought she might strike the child again, she remembered my saying that it was no one's fault. She went to the far end of the back yard where she couldn't hear the crying. (I imagined her filling her lungs with the rich pungency of earth and shrubbery, trying to breathe in patience.) If only Brian would even pretend to love his child, she said, but he wouldn't even look at her. And, no, Brian would not consider speaking to me.

When Amanda's sixth birthday arrived, Helen made a cake and lit six little candles. She said, "Blow them out, Amanda. Blow them out. You know how." Amanda got down from the table and walked away. Helen had to blow them out herself. She went to the grocery store and bought a bottle of wine. She had to cut the cork out with a knife because they did not have a corkscrew. Brian came home and asked why she was sleeping while Amanda was crying. They had another argument.

Time dragged without the lessons. She mended Amanda's clothes and sewed name-tapes on them. In the dreary afternoons she tried to nap while the child screamed until she was hoarse and crashed pot lids and toys on the coffee table.

At last she was told there was a place open for Amanda. She recounted to me the conversation she had with Brian.

He had responded, "Good. I told you ages ago to put her in a Home for kids like her."

"Are you saying, 'I told you so'?"

"I'm pissed off that you wasted all this time."

"I can't help that. I had to try, Brian."

"If it's what you want to do, just do it."

"I will."

Helen, looking away from me then, seemed to be seeing their argument again on an invisible screen.

"They may be able to give her what you can't. It may be for the best," I said. After a moment I asked her again, "Is it really what you want to do?"

She assured me, "Yes, it is."

*

It was a pale highveld morning when I waited for Helen at Little Eden. She left the bus carrying Amanda's suitcase in one hand and holding the child's hand with the other. Little Eden had the required reports, one from the Children's Hospital and the other from me.

Miss Blair met us. "I'll show you two around. Nanny will take care of Amanda."

We walked along the linoleum-tiled floors, a faint smell of urine lingering in the corridors. The neat four-bed rooms were furnished with brightly-coloured curtains and bedspreads. In one of them, a painfully thin teen-aged boy, lying in a crib with the sides up, turned his sucking mouth toward us.

While the wordless voices of children reached me from another part of the building, we walked to the sunlit dining room. Empty plastic plates and mugs lay on the breakfast-spattered plastic tablecloths. A uniformed nanny was still feeding a young girl, who turned her head toward the spoon like a blind mole and trembled at every touch.

In one of the shiny white bathrooms, children lined up to use the toilets. When it was Amanda's turn, she refused to stay seated on the porcelain rim of the toilet, its wooden seat tilted upright.

I said, "The porcelain is cold for children to sit on." The nanny banged the seat down angrily, and Amanda sat.

At the end of the morning, Miss Blair told Helen, "Amanda can stay if you wish."

"It is what I wish."

"All right. Let her settle down and come and see her in about two weeks."

Outside Little Eden, Helen said, "Miss Blair thinks I should be sad, but I feel nothing."

It was much longer than two weeks before she went back to see Amanda.

*

A month later, I drove to Little Eden for the follow-up visit. Miss Blair reported, "Amanda seems to be settling down. She didn't eat at all the first week, but now she's eating well. She threw a lot of tantrums then, too. She seems to be spoilt, to have got her own way too much. These children need firmness. Her mother must have spent a lot of time with her; she won't get that sort of individual attention here."

I tried not to let my face show my disappointment.

Miss Blair continued, "She likes to be hugged and cuddled, but—." She shrugged. "Come. The children are in the garden."

Children were scattered on the fenced lawn around the sandpit and play equipment. Three lay dozing on the grass in the mild sunshine; none of the others were interacting. While Miss Blair and I watched, Amanda picked up two handfuls of sand and opened her hands over her head. "Nice. Nice," she said and smiled while sand tumbled from her shining dark hair down over her glowing face. "Nice. Nice."

Amanda walked to within a few paces of Miss Blair and said without expression, "Toilet. Toilet."

Miss Blair commented, "She says that just to get attention."

Amanda walked off, picked up a large twig. "Stick. Stick." Still repeating the word, she walked around the lawn several times. She fell when her foot slipped off the grass at its circular edge near the tree. She got up and again approached Miss Blair. "Sore. Sore." She did not come closer or make eye contact or seem to expect comforting. She wandered off and, while reaching for another handful of sand, noticed a yellow bead. She picked it up and presented it to me, saying, "Thank you. Thank you."

I said, "Thank you, Amanda. It's a pretty bead." Amanda had seen me many times before, but there was no sign of recognition in the child's face. Was she autistic and not good socially or was she brain damaged and retarded? I might never know.

At lunchtime, Amanda was the first child in the dining room. She went to the wrong chair. Taken to her own chair and lifted onto it, she said, "Sit. Sit." After waiting for a while, she banged her forehead on the edge of the table. Her face reddened but showed no emotion. Impatient at waiting again, she turned to look at a parakeet in a cage behind her, looked across the table at me and said, "Bird. Bird."

"Yes, it's a bird," I responded.

Amanda turned to the window and pointed. "Bird! Bird!" she said loudly.

"Yes," I said. "Birds are outside, too. And flying."

The other children assembled for lunch. Amanda paid them no attention. The microcephalic boy on my left said, "Do you like fire engines? I like fire engines. I don't want to eat here. I want to eat in the garden."

"I would like to be outside too," I said truthfully.

The girl on my right said nothing, seeming to be unaware of everything, but when Miss Blair said, "Let us sing grace," she placed her hands together in front of her.

"For what we are receiving, let us give thanks . . ." sang the adults.

Amanda, still looking out at the birds, did not appear to be listening.

*

Jean Stewart's report to the university must have counted for more than Dr. Wallace's. My husband and four children came to my graduation in Pretoria at the end of 1974.

Mental Health Society
February 1975 – July 1979

Our Mental Health

My first job as a social worker was in Johannesburg from February 1975 to July 1979. It was at the Mental Health Society of the Witwatersrand (the White Waters Ridge). I was responsible for about a hundred clients jointly with the psychiatrist and psychiatric nurses. I counselled clients, applied for and administered state pensions, and supervised and trained social work students.

The word "Society" in Mental Health Society sounds friendly and homogenous, but all eight of us social workers judiciously kept our political opinions to ourselves in front of Mevrou (Mrs.) J. P. Joubert, the director. We were sure she voted for the Afrikaner Nationalist Party or even the further right party, the *Afrikaner Weerstandsbeweging*, the Afrikaner Resistance Movement, whose leader had adopted Hitler's fascist salute and whose emblem was the reverse swastika. We whispered among ourselves that Mevrou's parents had wanted a boy, which was why they had given her two boy's first names that we could not say out loud, which was why we always used her title.

The policy of "separate development" meant that we, the social workers, were governed by the three separate government Departments of Health, Welfare and Pensions, one each for "Whites," "Coloureds" (people of mixed race) and "Natives" (or blacks).

Social workers could deal only with clients in our own race category. We made home visits to clients, the mentally handicapped, as they were called then, and the mentally disturbed. Were they taking their meds? Did they need referrals? It made a kind of crazy sense for us to deal with our own race groups because decades of separation meant that each group had a different culture. The amount of government pensions and grants for clients differed, most money for whites, less for coloureds, and least for blacks. The amount of government subsidies for social workers' salaries differed in a similar way, which we did not talk about.

Christine Moya and Ann Ramaphosa went to clients in Soweto and Alexandra, black dormitory townships. One would think that Ann and Christine would be friends, but they weren't; perhaps they were from different tribes. Or perhaps Ann did not like Christine's ostensible policy of going along with the system. (Later, adherents of the African National Congress and Inkatha, the party of the Zulus, would kill each other in the run-up to the democratic elections.)

Barbara Watson, whose skin was light brown, wasn't friends with any of us and was often bad-tempered. That could have been because she was classified as "Coloured" and her people were rejected by both blacks and whites. She went to clients in Lenasia and Eldorado Park, areas set aside for "Coloureds."

The fact that "Coloureds" in America would be called blacks, no matter how light-skinned they were, was puzzling to us. In return, so we were told, some American tourists were befuddled by restrooms labeled "Coloureds" that did not have toilets and hand-basins in pastel colours but white ones, the same as in restrooms labeled "Whites." Previously, restrooms at airports were required to be relabeled "Whites" and "Non-Whites" because Americans, on having to choose between "European" and "Non-European," would choose the entrances that identified them as not coming from Europe—quite the opposite of what was intended. The explanation for the quaint wording at airports was that whites who settled in South Africa were overwhelmingly from Europe and were called Europeans.

"Coloureds" not only included people of mixed black and white heritage but Indians, Chinese, and Malays, who were also separately classified. The Japanese were trading partners and were classified as "honourary Whites." For reasons unknown to me, Malays would have to be reclassified if they moved from where they were living to even across the street. One could be classified as "Native" if a pencil stuck in one's hair did not fall out.

The Group Areas Act dictated where each race group could live and had employed forced removals to separate the races. The Immorality Act dictated that one could not have sexual relations with a person of another race. These Acts were factors in people's decisions to change their racial classification. In addition, the authorities used them to impose changes, some of which had devastating consequences. A child could be removed from its biological parents because of the child's appearance.

In one year alone, 1,176 people changed their racial classification, according to Michael Chapman in his concrete poem, "The Chameleon Dance." The majority had applied to become registered as lighter skinned than before, although nineteen whites became coloureds and twenty coloureds turned into blacks.

The five of us white social workers were assigned to "White" areas, north, south, east, west and central in the city of Johannesburg, and we were friends. Glenda Marks, Brenda Katz, Vivienne Budlender and I were northern suburb married women, who didn't actually need to be employed but chose to be. Glenda, Brenda and Vivienne were Jewish; Vaughan Edwards and I were not. Vaughan was a flaming queen, as he would be the first to tell you. He knew that he would never rise to become a director, as other male social workers speedily did. I later took over a private practice that Vaughan had in partnership with a friend who was leaving the country.

The five of us liberals could talk together about politics when sure of not being overheard. We were pleased to be involved in a multi-racial organization, a safe step in the right direction. As political activists we would have risked the banging on the door at two in the morning and imprisonment without trial for years, or at the least being confined to house arrest. We didn't ask the other three if they were activists. If they were arrested, it would be better not to be able to testify against them. I was not a South

African citizen, unlike the rest of my family, and would have been deported if arrested. I could not face the prospect of being separated from my four children.

Liberals were not popular with the right, understandably, nor with the left, as a poem by Christopher van Wyk (died January 2015), published in 1976, illustrated. His poem advised readers to beware of white ladies who plant flowers in black townships because this charity could make them overlook the need for equality and liberation

But I did not regret the tree I had planted with my friend Eleanor to provide shade for a bare beaten-earth playground at a school in Lenasia township, and I tried to be hopeful that someone, a teacher, parent or student, had watered the sapling.

The Censorship Board was vigilant, and newspapers were published with news items blacked out. This Board was also responsible for banning books that would be bad for our morals, so much so that people were more than ready to believe the urban legend that it banned Black Beauty on the basis of its title, without reading it. A member of the Board had said, "People have the silly idea that there must be freedom of the press and no repression. They don't realise that ideas are also a source of evil."

Dr. Albert Hertzog, former Minister of Posts and Telegraphs, had warned regarding television that "the effects of the wrong programmes on children, the less developed and other races can be destructive."

His government had not wanted us to know how the rest of the world saw South Africa and had vowed that we would never have a little *bioscope* (or cinema) in our sitting-rooms. Consequently, television arrived belatedly in the country, in January 1976—two decades behind most of the developed world.

The massive landmark concrete tower, from which television programmes were then broadcast to the nation, had been built to transmit FM radio signals and had been named the Hertzog Tower. With a sense of embarrassment, the authorities renamed it the SABC Tower.

Six months later, on 16 June, the Soweto riots exploded and were televised. The government had decreed that half of all black high school subjects would be taught in the hated language of the oppressors, never mind that few black teachers were sufficiently fluent in Afrikaans. Black students rioted.

In the rioting that day, Dr. Melville Edelstein, who had made a point of understanding young blacks' aspirations and had pleaded for more sympathetic treatment, heard of the uprising and went to his office, where he was stoned to death by the very youths he had tried to help.

Hector Pietersen was the first of twenty-four students to die by police bullets on that first day of rioting. They were shot when forty-eight policemen, forty of them black, were surrounded by 6,000 rioting black students. The now iconic photo of Hector's body carried by a weeping fellow student was on the front page of the *Rand Daily Mail* and was fresh in our minds at the time of the staff meeting on Friday afternoon.

"Are there any problems anyone wants to raise?" asked Mevrou Joubert.

Ann Ramaphosa jumped to her feet. I had never seen her so angry. "I want to protest about the segregated toilets in these offices. Are all you lily-white liberals afraid your bums will turn black if I sit on the same toilet as you?"

The five of us sat and looked at our toes. We hadn't even thought of trying to desegregate the toilets.

I cannot tell you what Mevrou did because I was too embarrassed to look up.

*

In 1960 British Prime Minister Harold MacMillan had referred to the "Wind of Change" that was blowing down Africa. Country after country to the north, colonized by European nations, became self-governing, and that "wind" blew ever closer.

Libya had first gained independence in 1951, then the Sudan in 1956 and the Gold Coast, as Ghana, in 1957. Most of the other countries followed between 1956 and 1962. Then it was the turn of Angola and Mozambique in 1974, just two years previously. That left only Zimbabwe and Namibia standing between the rest of the continent and South Africa.

In 1976, when the Department of Bantu Affairs (or Native Affairs) was renamed the Department of Plural Relations and Development, irrepressible Ann Ramaphosa again stood up in a staff meeting. She solemnly announced, "I am here to tell you that I am not a Plural" Political blasphemy! But since the times in South Africa were beginning to change, Mevrou could only look at her blandly.

Simplicity

The air was heavy with antiseptic and anaesthetic. It caught in Donald's lungs, already irritable from his walk from the bus stop in the morning chill. He was afraid that the pungent smell would set off a fit of useless coughing and it would go on and on and leave him exhausted. He sat himself down on one of the orange and black moulded plastic chairs near the entrance of the Johannesburg General Hospital and forced himself to take small even breaths until his normal rhythm of breathing returned.

The place was beginning to fill up: he would have to move to the front of the waiting room to claim an early place in the queue.

It would be easier if Ella were still here, Ella who had always been his strength.

"You can do it," her remembered voice said. That was when he had been offered a promotion, more authority, responsibility for a section, a hundred men, and when confidence had left him. But he *had* managed before he was invalided out. The girls could be a help now, if they would. The walking and the bus journey took it out of him more and more. They were busy with their families, and he did not want to lay claim to their concern with his prognosis: "We can stabilize your condition, but we can't cure you." The medicines were not helping. He had given up smoking, but fumes and dust continued the damage. Would it be possible to get away from the city?

An urgent need to escape from his thoughts made him rise and concentrate on his careful way to the front row of chairs. It was not yet full: he could be seen this morning, perhaps even before the staff tea break.

There was something strange about the figure of the young man next to him in the row of seats. His small dark cropped head was turned away and the stocky tweed-jacketed body leaned out, twisted at the waist so that its owner could look at the waiting patients ahead of him. Donald glanced down at heavy brogues, navy blue trousers, and a smooth white hand with tapering fingers that stood out against the blue knee of the trousers.

As though feeling the curious stare, the young man leaned back and turned to look at him. Startled by unexpectedly diminutive features, Donald exclaimed, "Oh, you're a woman! Why do you dress like a man?"

"I walk," she answered evenly. "I walk all over the place and at night. Nobody gives me any trouble dressed like this."

"Oh," he said, embarrassed by the grossness of his question. Wanting safer ground, he added gruffly, "Why are you here? You look healthy enough."

"I had 'flu, and they said I should come back next week. They don't like it if you don't keep appointments. Why are you here?"

The habit of keeping his condition to himself was strong. "A spot of chest trouble."

Pale blue eyes set in an unlined face continued to look steadily into his own. Anxious to avoid another question, he went on hurriedly, "I was thinking how good it would be to get away from the city, to live somewhere where there are trees and hills and perhaps a stream nearby." He gave a short laugh. "Back to nature, you know."

"Yes, I know. I walk to the green places. I've seen the sun come up at Zoo Lake."

Her answer took him seriously and affirmed his yearning. He began to play aloud with possibilities. "I've enough money saved for a second-hand caravan.* Terry, my son-in-law, could tow it out. He and I could spend a day or a weekend looking for the right place. It would need to be near enough to a town so I could go in and draw my pension and do the shopping."

*caravan: camper trailer

He fell silent, thinking of catching buses and of walking on a dirt road with passing cars churning up dust and his chest catching and heaving.

She remained still, with an air of timelessly waiting for him while he mourned his dream alone.

Then her voice recalled him, "I'm on a pension, too," and continued as if she had read his thoughts, "I could bring the pension money and groceries from the town." She went on looking him full in the face, and he searched for guile, sounding for a shifting of shadows in the depths of her clearwater eyes.

"What are you saying?"

"I'm saying I could come with you. I used to work as a nurse-aid. You're not well. I could look after you."

He felt weak, dazed by the unreality, the impact of her statements. His revived vision of pure air in the grove and the splash of running stream on stones clashed with his distrust.

"What do you want with an old man like me!" The words were torn out of him. Faces turned in his direction, and in the corner of his eye white uniforms halted in their progress. She continued to look at him directly, impassively, her small square jaw tilted up to his face, eyes fixed patiently on his, seeming not to blink in their waiting.

More gently, he asked, "What do you want with me?"

She sighed. "My parents and my brother don't want me to come round when there are visitors, so I don't go at all, but I miss them. I want to belong to you."

It came to him. The pension, her not working, and her naivety: she was simple, that was it, not a girl up to mischief. An image of her in the caravan came to him. She was preparing a meal, going contentedly about her work, absorbed in the quiet run of her limited thoughts, leaving him in peace to his reveries. Would it matter when he wanted to talk that she would hear without comprehending everything? Would she bore him with prattle? She didn't seem the kind to prattle, but, anyway, maybe, maybe all that was a small price to pay for the comfort of another being when the coughing took him at night and he struggled against drowning in his own fluid. But, what would people think? What would his daughters think?

Her uninflected voice broke in on him. "You will grow to love me."

"Yes," he answered, "I think so."

Mr. Arthur's Rocket

Sister Glover came into the cloakroom. My hands and arms were red from scrubbing with liquid soap from the dispenser. I had been trying to get rid of the smell, but it hadn't come off. It was all over me. I wanted to wash my hair and change my clothes too.

"What's up with you?" she asked, and I told her about Mr. Arthur and the mortuary and the smell I had picked up.

"It's the smell of death," she said. "Sometimes it's the first you know they've gone. It'll wear off."

She breezed out, and I was left wondering why the smell of death should be so sweet, so powerful and so unbearable. I wasn't ready for this in my first job as a social worker at the Mental Health Society of the Witwatersrand in Johannesburg.

*

That morning, a voice on the phone—the abrupt, slightly guttural voice of an official—had asked, "Do you know Mr. E. C. Arthur?"

"He's one of my clients," I admitted cautiously. I was always cautious with officials.

"He's dead. Where are his relatives staying?"

"He has no relatives. We're his guardians. What's happened?"

"There was an accident with a bus by the Landrost Hotel. He is at the Germiston Mortuary. You must send somebody as soon as possible to identify the body."

I checked with St. Elizabeth's Hostel, where he lived. They had been told. I found myself staring mindlessly at the hessian covering the partition in front of my desk. Then I remembered the way Mr. Arthur walked—with only his destination in mind, never looking left or right. He would have stepped in front of the bus. Quick. Instant. But the bus driver: awful for him. There would be an Inquiry. They should be told it wasn't the driver's fault. The passengers would have been distressed too. It would not have happened if Mr. Arthur had been kept confined in an institution. He would have been safe. It was his mother's fault.

The official's voice returned like an echo. "Germiston. You must send somebody." All right. I'll send somebody. One of the clinic sisters. Medical training. They knew about death. Death is physical, not social, nothing to do with social work. The clinic had a file on Mr. Arthur. But theirs was a slim file, not a bulging one like the one in my cabinet. They would tell me it's not a medical matter, no more to be done medically: it's your case now.

I knew Sister Glover would go with me to the mortuary if she was free, but she'd already told me she wasn't. I walked through the whole clinic and past all the social workers' offices, looking into open doors, with the foolish hope that I might find someone with nothing to do but accompany me. I consulted the map. Germiston was unknown territory—out in the *bundu*—when you lived in Johannesburg.

In the staff car on the way to the mortuary, I kept seeing Mr. Arthur's tall, thin, gangling figure walking along Jeppe Street in his single-minded way. Why was I sad? He was only one of a hundred or so cases. His image came to me clearer and closer: aquiline, strangely vacant features. Newly washed and shaved, as always. Dressed neatly and formally, as always, in the brown herring-bone tweed suit he wore even in the height of summer with a brown felt hat and newly-shined shoes. No one called him by his first name; I couldn't recall what it was.

Stepping in front of a bus was so pointless. I had never met his mother, but I could see it was her years of patient training that accounted for his ways. I could imagine the hard life she'd had because she didn't put him in a Home but kept him with her, even after her husband died and she had to manage on her own. Although Mrs. Arthur had taught him a lot, the lesson about looking left and right had not sunk in. He wasn't supposed to cross roads on his own. What would she think now about her decision to leave him out in the wide world?

Sister Glover had popped into my office just before I left for Germiston. "People will remember him," she said. "Remember how he liked to run errands, how he was always asking to be sent somewhere so he could feel useful? Remember the way he was always saying, 'My mother was a good woman.'? Remember what he said that day in clinic?"

I did remember. That day he was sitting in the crowded waiting room while staff bustled in and out of the consulting rooms. Mr. Arthur called out, "Sister! Sister!" When Sister Glover stopped and looked at him he said loudly, "Sister, my willy is hard. When I look at Mrs. Cohen's chest my willy goes hard."

Faces had frozen; no one blinked. "That's all right," Sister Glover told him. "Go for a walk. But just around the block. I want to see you back here in fifteen minutes. Mind what I say now."

We found it funnier than it really was. That happened sometimes when the realization that you weren't making a dent in all the cases you were responsible for struck you.

Mr. Arthur saw the psychiatrist every week. He got medication because of his anger. And because he couldn't say why he was angry, he could be violent and the staff couldn't handle him. But the medication made him seem wooden, not real, robotic.

*

I had located the mortuary in the grounds of Germiston Hospital. It was a small building, like the old brick and tin-roofed miners' houses, set apart, hidden away in a corner of the grounds behind a hedge and stand of trees.

A young uniformed policeman—not the doctor in a white coat I had expected—opened the door. He sat me down at a corner of his desk to fill in a form. He studied the form in silence after I signed and dated it then put it aside with a small sigh. Not looking at me, he said, "Just wait a few minutes while I get everything ready."

His footsteps grew fainter. Strain my ears as much as I could, I heard nothing. Time went by. What could he be doing? I remembered my nightmares about death years ago, after two of my classmates drowned. I was on my feet, about to leave, when the policeman was back, blocking the doorway.

"Come," he said and applying the pressure of firm fingers above my elbow led me out of the office. We walked down a corridor of Public Works walls, glossy dark green paint halfway to the ceiling and cream the rest of the way up. Damp rose from the concrete floor. Low wattage light from one naked light globe did not reach the corners. The policeman stopped me near a small window high on one wall. He pulled a curtain aside and beckoned me to approach. The room on the other side of the window was bright; three white walls and a ceiling gleamed.

"Can you see?" he asked. I was too short or the window was too high for me to see what he wanted me to see. I looked at him mutely, still wanting to run.

"Come," he said again and let the curtain fall. I followed him around a corner and through a door. With courteous hands, he positioned me at the side of a high bed. A man lay on it with a sheet up to his chin and a small white cloth over the top of his head.

It *is* his mustache, I thought, and it *is* his bony nose with a bump on it from an old break like my father's nose. But it isn't his forehead, not at all his forehead, with a ridge above the eyebrows like that. All this way for nothing. But perhaps they took the top of his skull off and didn't fit it back on again properly. That would explain it. That's what could happen when you weren't around to look after yourself.

"Is it him?" came the low voice of the policeman. Mr. Arthur's face swam back into focus. "Is it?" his voice insisted.

"Yes."

Fingers, moth-like on my arm, turned me away and out through the doorway. "Are you all right?" Concern in his voice. He must have difficult times in this job of his and be lonely in the mortuary with only the dead for company.

Outside, leaning against the staff car, I retched again and again till nothing came up. It was the sickening way Mr. Arthur's body was different: empty, impossible to be lived in again.

Driving back to the office, I wondered, not for the first time, what happened after people died. My friend Sandy said there was no doubt souls would find happiness ultimately. But Sandy believed in a mish-mash of things, like both purgatory and reincarnation. I told her it was more scientific to think the soul was energy that couldn't just disappear but went into trees and rocks and clouds like Wordsworth's Lucy. Could trees and rocks and clouds be happy?

You shouldn't cry while driving on the freeway, so I concentrated on the road and tried not to think.

Back in the office, I got some files up to date for the weekly supervision meeting, and then I was just sitting when Sister Glover came in.

"Was it Mr. Arthur?" she asked.

"Yes."

"You won't be any use to the others if you let it get to you."

"I know that," I said. I scowled at her, and she went away.

I went on just sitting, empty and calm, at my desk until the thought leapt into my mind that there would have to be a funeral and I would have to arrange it. People from his hostel would go, and the women he sat among at daily devotions at his church would probably go. One or two nurses from the clinic might too, if they could be spared. Would anyone really care? Mr. Arthur had no social skills and no "relationship capacity," as we called it. He never spoke to the other patients, just stared straight ahead, even if they always came to the clinic on the same day. He was like a shadow, living on the outskirts of society, not making a difference, not interested in making the world a better place. But someone should grieve, and it seemed that I was elected, so I let the tears come.

After a while, I called the funeral parlour. "No," the voice said adamantly. "No, you will have to come in. There are forms to fill in for authorisation. It's regulations. Anyone can call, you know, and say someone is dead, even for a joke."

That night I was asleep when my head hit the pillow. In the morning, the gravel path in Braamfontein grated underfoot, loud in the serene garden of velvet-pile grass, broken only by perfect circles of earth in which stood standard roses, all identical in height, equidistant from each other and orderly, seeming to deny the disorder of death.

A white-coated woman opened the door of Doves Funeral Parlour. She motioned me to follow her along a corridor of thick carpets, so thick that my feet sank into then as I walked. Still without speaking, she pointed to a chair in an empty office before disappearing. Her silence was proper in the circumstances; it must show reverence. I wished I had a cigarette, but it wouldn't be reverent to smoke. Besides, there was no ashtray.

From beyond the door came a susurration like wind in trees and a vague murmuring of faraway voices. Perhaps the thick carpets and the acoustic bumps on the ceiling were muffling and distorting sounds. There was also a strange smell. Maybe it was formalin. Formalin kept bodies the way they were so people could imagine that the friend or relative they had come to see was still here and knew they had come to say good-bye.

I wished Mr. Arthur had family who were here instead of me. He was still lying on a trolley in that cold and damp mortuary. He had to be put to rest in the holding earth; that was what was important, and that was my job now. If I breathed in and out and said "One" through my nose on each out-breath in a reverberating kind of way, like an Eastern mystic, I would be able to go on with it. I was humming the second "One" when a man came into the room, so I changed it to clearing my throat.

Like the woman who had opened the door, the man's eyes were cast down. Bent forward and dressed in a dark dress-suit with tails, he resembled a beetle. He stopped in front of me and bowed still lower, then stood erect with his hands cuddling each other like courting doves.

I extended my own hand, and one of his doves left the other and came forward. A warm damp impression remained on my palm while the doves again rounded on each other, pliant and stroking.

"I am Mr. Nightingale. Please let me offer my sympathy."

That couldn't be his real name. It was probably something like Jones. Was I supposed to think of a nightingale singing in Berkeley Square? He sat on his side of the desk and pushed a form toward me. Once again, I filled in the spaces. When I reached the space at the bottom for rands and cents, I asked, "What does a funeral cost, the price range, I mean?"

"How much is available for the deceased?" he countered.

"Not much. In fact, this month's pension should go back because he died before the pay-out date."

"The bottom line is a pauper's funeral. No trimmings."

That was what I ought to choose, but Mrs. Arthur presented herself to me in a corner of the ceiling, floating up there like a whale. She was glowering at the word "pauper." She folded her arms under her ample bosom and pressed her lips together. I understood that she hadn't had spare cash to take out a funeral policy for her son.

"We don't want a pauper's funeral," I told Mr. Nightingale, "and not the one up from that. The next one up, what does that cost?"

I filled in the figure he told me on the form. As I signed it, I hoped there was enough left in Mr. Arthur's account. Otherwise, I could take up a collection at work. If that wasn't enough, I would have to take the rest out of my savings account. I felt a hot surge of anger toward Mrs. Arthur.

"What relationship are you to the deceased?" Mr. Nightingale asked.

"I'm not related. I'm only his social worker."

He looked at me appraisingly. Did he think I had been deceiving him? Long seconds passed, then he cheered up, his back straightened and his doves became hands. I had a glimpse of him as a man who ate oatmeal porridge in the morning and slurped his tea.

"Well, my dear," he began, "then you will understand. You wouldn't believe the trouble I have with staff. They don't want to learn the business from the ground up like I did."

He began to laugh, and he laughed so much that he lost his breath and had a coughing fit. When his breath returned he began to explain his joke, "The ground up, see? The basement is where the bodies are brought in, see, and where the work on them is done. The ones that want to come into the business today can't take that. But it's the only way—from the ground up. And another trouble is that them that *can* take it haven't got the brains for the administration side. Do you get my drift?"

Undertaking is a dying art, I thought, but I got a grip on myself before I said it out loud.

Problem-solving, a method of social work, had started to come automatically, but I could see it was no use telling him that times had changed. He was enjoying expounding to an audience of one. Maybe he hadn't had that experience in his career for a while or forever.

He stood up and smiled. "Let me show you the display room."

It was peculiar that the somber role he had previously put on was for the benefit of relatives and not out of respect for the bodies.

"Thank you, Mr. Nightingale, but I must get back to the office now."

"It won't take a minute. Come along." His eyes were wide, shining like black olives. I couldn't disappoint him now that he looked just like a boy before his fifth birthday party.

We walked along another carpeted corridor to a door at the end. After he opened it we were standing in a very large room. A row of coffins lined the wall on our left. That row was separated by a walkway from rows and rows of coffins stretching away to the far right end of the room.

Mr. Nightingale bounded forward past the plain pine coffins on the left. He came to a halt and pointed to a group of long boxes on our right covered with thick, dark, opaque varnish, obviously meant to make the cheap pine underneath look like more expensive wood. He didn't comment but bounced on the spot with what seemed suppressed excitement.

Almost at once, he swept me off and guided me to the end of that row and around to the next row on the right. As we proceeded in this way—Mr. Nightingale springing along and me at a half trot—the wood of the coffins grew more lustrous and their handles changed from chrome to brass to silver-plate and then to what looked like real sterling silver.

Mr. Nightingale stopped and looked at me, seeming to ask for comment. He was in front of a coppery-red coffin with a whorled and whirling grain, polished smooth as butter, with gold handles. Could they actually be gold?

"Beautiful," I said. "I didn't know how much craftsmanship went into this sort of thing."

He beamed with pleasure. "I want to show you the Chinese coffins." Off to a small group against the end wall we hurried. These coffins were wider than usual, splendours lined with deep soft cushions covered by white satin, sirens of coffins to seduce with a song: *Come and rest; take your ease; you have laboured long.*

I wondered what Mr. Arthur would make of the Chinese coffins. He was conservative like his mother.

"White is the colour for funerals for the Chinese," Mr. Nightingale commented. "They believe death should be celebrated."

I tried to think of Mr. Arthur's death as a celebration while Mr. Nightingale led on at a slower pace. Mr. Arthur's life wasn't one to celebrate. He would never have had a job or got married or had children or a more full life.

Mr. Nightingale said over his shoulder, "This is the best. I've kept it for last." He stopped a short distance before a large gleaming stainless steel shape in the corner of the room. It was cylindrical, with a pointed end and a flat base, looking for all the world like a rocket that had lost its way and had come to rest upright in this warehouse of coffins.

Face aglow, Mr. Nightingale looked back and forth from his "best" to my face.

"It's a rocket," I said.

He laughed uproariously, enjoying my stupefaction, and went on laughing, holding his sides, which people only did in books.

"No," he gasped at last, "it's a coffin really. Last forever it will and, see, when the departed is inside it's hermetically sealed. Nothing can get in or out. Imported from America. Costs ten thousand rand. We don't get much call for them."

He took me round to the back of it to show me its special attraction: a metal tube that could be removed from the base of the rocket-coffin and opened, then closed again and replaced, and finally sealed shut.

"What would you put in it?" I asked him.

He shrugged, disappointed by my lack of imagination. "Valuables. Relics of today. A message . . ."

Trailing behind him on the way out, it seemed to me that it would be better to have fuel with a fuse in the base of the rocket so it could whoosh away into the highest part of the sky.

Disappointed in me though he was, Mr. Nightingale shook my hand vigourously in the doorway. "You must come in again any time you're passing."

Outside Doves Funeral Parlour, I stood stunned for a few seconds while cars and trucks sped past on Jorissen Street. Then I burst out laughing, having held back laughter for a long time, and everything became clear. Mr. Arthur should have the ten thousand rand rocket—with fuel in the base to be ignited—and the rocket should have a window in it so Mr. Arthur wouldn't feel claustrophobic and he could see all of us who knew him waving and cheering during lift-off and we could all see him zooming away to explore the universe while he laughed and clapped his hands, not wooden, not robotic any more.

Freedom

Light bulbs set into the ceiling highlight the spotless bar counter and the array of bottles and glasses behind it. They also shine down on two men, one behind the bar with a white apron over his shirt and trousers, the other in front of it wearing a linen suit.

"Why weren't you here yesterday?" the man in the suit asks. The bartender continues to polish the glass he is holding and does not answer.

His employer's question floats in the room unbound by time while the bartender continues to polish the glass. Suddenly irritated, the other man's features twist. "Hell's teeth! Don't ignore me. Why weren't you here yesterday?"

"I have explained the situation to you," calmly replies the bartender. "Yesterday was the end of the month. You should have remembered that I would have exceeded my quota if I had worked yesterday. I have explained my requirements to you."

"Damn nonsense," splutters his employer. "Why don't you say when you're not coming? And, if you won't work when I need you, I'll find someone who will."

"Find someone then." An upsurge of spirit comes with his words. "Find someone who is a better employee, who doesn't drink, doesn't steal your profits. If you can. Keep your job. Stick it where it fits." He unties the tapes of the apron behind his waist, lifts the apron over his head and drops it. "Pay me what you owe, and I'll go."

His employer abruptly makes for the inner door, returns after a few minutes with a sheaf of banknotes and finds the barman standing where he left him. He extends the notes; the other takes and pockets them without a word and goes out of the old-time swing doors towards the main exit.

A muttered "Crazy" follows the retreating back. "To live like a pauper so as not to give the Receiver of Revenue his share. What kind of freedom is that?

The former bartender walks northward in the sunlight, his cuffs buttoned and his tieless shirt open at his throat. His hair, sleekly combed back, implies concealment of a bald patch, and sunlight reveals new growth of grey in the glinting redness. While walking he looks directly into the faces of the young women thronging the sidewalk during their lunch break. When they notice his stare, his seeking eyes, they avert their own. His pale skin takes on a freshly-bruised hue

"Am I a dog?" he mouths as he walks on. "Can't they respond to friendliness? Who do they think they are?"

At the sign, L. K. Jacobs & Co., Letting Agents, he climbs the few steps to the glass door with the buzzer beside it. Eyes check him briefly before a click announces that he can push the door open.

The woman at the desk flicks through papers. "You are in arrears. Two months."

"I will pay two months."

"You owe in advance. You owe three months."

"I will pay two months."

"You have an obligation to pay in advance. That is the condition. You are forever in arrears. If you don't pay in advance you'll have to be evicted."

"Have to be evicted, have to be evicted. I always pay. You always get the money. Here is the two months. You will get the rest later."

He waits. She glances heavenward and makes out a receipt.

He takes the receipt. "You can't put me out. It's rent controlled."

"We can if you don't pay. You know that."

*

A baby waits in a stroller while his mother peruses clothing in the window of O K Bazaars. The man stoops, squats on his haunches, smiles and looks into the baby's face. His gaze is solemnly returned.

"The eyes of babies are so straightforward, so trusting," he tells the mother who has turned away from the window. "They haven't been ruined yet by the world and its pretences."

The woman glares at him, seizes the rubber-covered handle firmly and zigzags away through the crowd.

"Bitch!" he says and watches her swinging hips and the long shapely line of her legs in retreat.

He crosses the road in the face of a sea of oncoming traffic and in the middle of the block turns in between green lettering on glass fronts. He examines dried fruit in trays.

"Can I help you?"

"Is this fruit preserved without chemicals?"

"Yes, it's chemical-free. Only sulphur is used on some of the fruit; otherwise it would turn black."

"Then, what do you mean it is chemical-free?"

"That is standard practice, sir. Other stores are lying to you if they say sulphur is not used."

"Then you deceive the public as well as rob them."

"What do you mean, sir?"

"Look at the prices of these vegetables; look at the price of the honey. You set yourselves up as benefactors providing uncontaminated food and you lie and rob the people."

"We are a speciality store; we don't buy in bulk like the chain stores."

"I don't believe you are not making outrageous profits."

"You are free to think so, sir."

Continuing his walk, he approaches an open air car park, where he notices an elderly woman struggling to throw a tarpaulin over the roof of a car. She throws a rope-ended corner up and over, but there is sufficient breeze to blow it back at her. Watching her efforts, he moves toward her, as if to help. At the entrance of the car park he becomes aware of a cluster of policemen examining the contents of the trunk of one of the other cars. He returns to the original path of his walk, quickening his pace.

A few blocks farther on, he crosses the road and enters a corner café, where he collects milk, cheese, bread and peanut butter after studying the prices on the articles. The man behind the counter rings up the prices on the till and tells him the total.

"It is not as much as that," he shouts. "I have calculated it."

"The price is with the tax added," comes the response.

The man considers this information and mentally calculates. He counts the money out onto his palm, transfers it to his right hand and throws it on the counter. Some of it falls on the floor.

"You should not be allowed to do that!" he rages. "Deceiving people. The price should be all-inclusive."

Fuming, he carries his purchases two blocks farther and walks into the entrance of a block of flats, from which the exterior paint is peeling.

*

A knock comes at his door. "Can I use your phone?" the brown-skinned woman asks.

He steps aside to let her in.

"I'll pay for the call."

He does not acknowledge her offer.

"Or," she begins hesitantly, "I could clean up a bit for you."

"Is the place dirty, then?" he barks.

"There is some dust." Her lowered head apologises.

"Dust! What's the use of stirring up dust, filling the air with it, moving it from place to place."

"I'll pay for the call," says the woman, and she moves to the telephone that rests on a dark sideboard standing on ball-and-claw feet.

He waits in the open doorway for her to finish her call. She places a coin on the embroidered cloth next to the telephone and sidles past him out of the doorway.

After closing the door, he stands in front of an easel holding a large piece of hardboard painted white. Other squares of hardboard lean against the wall with their brown backs facing into the room.

There is another knock at the door. He smiles at the tall blonde woman wearing heavy make-up. "After all. I didn't think you would come here again."

"I couldn't leave it unfinished. I thought I should tell you why. May I come in?"

She stops in her stride just inside the doorway. "Where is the lounge suite?"

"I sold it. I needed the money. Anyway, one should not be attached to material things."

She sits on a fold-up bed, made of foam cushions. It is open and covered with disarrayed bed linen.

"Some material things come under the heading of necessities," she observes drily. "But I came to tell you why I won't see you again. I thought on first meeting that you were an interesting man with potential as an artist, but as I've got to know you better, I've seen that I could never adjust to your lifestyle."

Without turning his gaze from his blank "canvas," he says with sudden heat, "That's the trouble with you: your bourgeois values."

"My values! It's the lack of sense in yours I object to. Look at you. You resent any restriction on your freedom. You reduce yourself to poverty because you don't want to give anything to anyone—not to the government, not to you ex-wife—and you've put yourself in a position where everyone else is in the wrong because you feel unjustly deprived."

"You understand nothing with your northern suburbs mentality," he rejoins.

"I understand that you have nothing to offer me. I understand that you make grand gestures and that the grand gesture of burning your ID document means you have to skulk when you see a policeman. Do you think any woman would want to skulk with you?"

"You are free to make whatever choice you want."

"It's not a difficult choice. What can you offer me? Sex and perhaps reflected glory when you make it as an artist."

"You must admit I'm good at it—sex, I mean. Tell you what: I've got some cash left. I'll take you to High Point to play the slot machines."

"For you to run out of money and start borrowing even sooner? No thanks."

"I think you had better leave now."

"I will, but one last thing: you should stop your bullshit about cockroaches being clean creatures and get rid of them."

"Get out," he says with thinned lips.

*

He leaves his flat, slamming the Yale lock closed behind him. In the foyer of a tall office block, he scowls while he gouges his name and time of arrival on the register supervised by a guard.

Ten floors up, a harassed man replies, "It's all very well that your collection is ready, but what we need is your check. We simply can't, as you suggest, let you have exhibition space on credit . . . No we can't. You have to pay for the premises. Your art is experimental; it may not sell; we can't count on commission. Please understand that. No, you see, we can't. Let me be candid. The fact that you are an architect does not guarantee that you're an artist with general appeal. You may not have enough training as an artist: you have to understand the rules before you can break them."

*

Back in the flat he sits on the foam mattress and watches a ring of cockroaches. Nine of them—four darker and larger than the others appearing to be males—form a circle on the wall with their heads toward the center of the circle. They are still except for an occasional wave of antennae.

"My little ones, my pretty ones," he croons. "They don't know. It's just prejudice to say that you are dirty. You clean my kitchen. You nibble yourselves clean."

He reaches out a forefinger to stroke the nearest one and goes on crooning. "You are sensitive, you are kind, you are intelligent. Stay in peace, my pretty ones."

1978 – 1980

Dust

I added the receipt for the electricity connection to the small pile of documents: the other receipts, my savings book, and the precious new lease. They all rested on a pad of dust in the narrow space between two of the beams supporting the second storey. The dust could have been pulled out in a single piece like a strip of hairy grey felt.

I heard his cough at the foot of the stairs. My hand darted to the small plank and replaced it over my under-floor câche, and I quickly stood and bent again to roll the small Oriental rug over that ill-fitting plank that allowed tracking from feet and under-bed fluff to seep down.

My stockinged feet took me soundlessly across the floorboards to the window, where I leaned my face against the wrought-iron burglar bars to try to steady myself and to catch a breeze on my hot cheeks. I held on to one of its curves shaped like half a heart.

"What are you doing there?" he asked.

Did he suspect something? I said, "Just looking at the tree."

"Just looking at the tree?"

Why had I said that? I was babbling like an infant, sounds without meaning. "It has always been beautiful to see the tree from here. From this room. To see the birds in the leafy treetop ignoring us and just being birds." Babbling again. I hoped he did not think I was referring to his decision to cut the tree down because it made the back garden cold and dark. That was pointless now. I hoped he could hear my love of this room and my gratitude.

He hooked his thumbs under his belt and said, "What have you decided?" The light blue of his shirt was a darker blue in arcs under his armpits.

He stepped forward, stopped and stood on the rug that sheltered my secret. I glanced back at the tree, and before I turned to face him again I heard the wailing of women when news of death came. Was it now the time or would later be the time to wail?

He did not know that I could see the darker half-moons growing on his shirt, and I kept my gaze above them, lest he should be ashamed or lest I might be tempted to run and rest my head on that place below his shoulder where his heart had thumped on and on through the years and where I might take up the wet blue slackness of cloth and breathe in through it and hold it to my face and then press it against the silky skin next to his nipple and say, "Let's try again."

I could not think like that. The keys of the house would be with the owner, and I had signed, remember, signed an application for a telephone. What did the telephone matter? What was wrong with me?

"What have you decided?" he said again.

"What can be decided?" I tried to sound indifferent. "You say if I leave, I leave barefoot and without the children. Your lawyer says we should partition the house and live separately in it. That wouldn't work. What could a woman decide?"

The muscles in his face relaxed; his shoulders dropped slightly. How little he knew me still? How could he not guess? How could he not see that I was frail, having lost twenty pounds since the decision?

"If only you could be reasonable," he said, turning. "Why did you change? You used to be so sweet." He walked toward the door. His shoes thudded on the wooden stairs through the runner. The fifth stair creaked as usual. The front door closed.

*

I hold on to the wrought iron to take in the memory of its support for tomorrow. Let me sleep tonight to have a clear mind. Let me not wake in a cold sweat during the night, as usual. In the morning, so many things to remember, so many things to do after the usual car drop-off: Barbara at Parktown Girls School, Alan and Jocelyn at the university, and, finally, God willing, I will say good-bye to him when he gets out of the car to go to his office in the city centre.

Then back home, before my friends arrive to help pack, I must remember to remove his pistol from its hiding place in the wardrobe and put it in my handbag for safekeeping. He was ever-vigilant: smelling my fear, he might decide to return. Immeasurable rage. My friends possibly in danger. It must not happen.

The truck may need to make several trips with necessary furniture the lawyer said I could take to create a new home. Alan will return home, and with the gardener he will load the truck and drive it to our destination. Will he ever be forgiven?

At the end, before leaving, I will write the note I cannot think of writing without my life seeming to drain out of my body, the note that must be left on Jocelyn's desk. If only she had not turned her face away. If only I could have trusted her not to tell. If only he had not divided the family. Will she ever forgive me?

It had seemed impossible to break the bond between us; he and I were like reinforced concrete, he the cement and I the iron bars. To become my own person, I had needed to teach myself to hate him by cataloging his wrongs against me. Then I could wrench myself away.

Before I signed the lease, I saw a film of dust on the month-empty floors of the new house. It had flowed in through fanlight windows left open to keep the air sweet, and it lies on the wax patina of the parquet floors. When the children are settled for the night I will begin. I will take a feather duster from the carrier bag of soon needed things. On my knees, I'll make wide crescent sweeps of my arms with the duster and then shake the duster outside the back door. After a while, the floor will shine free of dust and the grain of the floor-boards show up again.

Sailing Away

I set out in the small rowboat, loaded to my gills, about to sink under the burden. My small craft filling with water, I jettisoned eating my sentences, minding my ayes to zees, zipping my teeth closed, and three bags full, sir. The sea grew rough. Oh, the turmoil and tempest! I flotsammed security and inheritance and worth-more-dead-than-alive. The consequent murderous temptation then had to go, along with jealousy and suspicion and house turned into prison. Black clouds loomed. I scooped pettiness and fear from the gunnels and dribbled them over the side into the choppy white water. My boat pitched and rolled. I tossed overboard duty and traditional roles and patriarchy. After them flowed cheeseparing, ants in the pantry, and my ducks in a row. The water-level in the dinghy subsided slightly. I jetsammed dreariness with fidelity and adultery and the bullet that missed my head. Giant waves raised themselves up, curved and crashed. My tears when preparing the obligatory sack of onions for pickling yearned to merge with the waves. Overboard and into the deep they went, and into the darkness of the deep also went control and complaints. Half-crazed, while the sea heaved, I bailed for my life, bailed for hours, bailed failure, disappointment, afterthoughts, and yesterdays' regrets. Lawyers' fees followed. My sailing dory rode higher on the waves. Lastly—I thought—I discarded solicitor and barrister and the long-awaited decree. Evening was coming on, but the day grew lighter. Still I scooped with bare hands, raw fingers, pursuing shards, fragments, consigning every last splinter to full fathoms five my marriage lies. Finally, finally, a fair wind blew, the foresail filled—a great white half-balloon—and my yacht and I went skimming high on wave tops, flying free toward tomorrow.

First Aid

Mark turned away from the Moon Rover machine at the Greek café. He had hoped his tour of the small Parkwood shopping center would provide more of interest, something, anything. But nothing had changed since the previous boarding school holidays. He was now out of twenty-cent pieces and his friends in the neighbourhood were still in school. Next holidays, when he went to his father it would be just as bad with friends from boarding school living far away.

That was their solution: boarding school and alternate holidays with them, so he wouldn't be living with either of them. That was fair, they had said.

The black guy who had been playing side-by-side at the next machine had also run out of money. The café was empty except for the owner, leaning on his elbow, watching his small black and white television set, waiting for customers, waiting for the day to pass.

It was a civilised divorce, they said; it wouldn't affect his life much. Not much! It was all arranged for him: boarding school, custody, access. Friends he asked said their parents argued too but made up. Why couldn't they do that instead of trying to make him think they weren't arguing? Did they think he couldn't hear loud voices behind the closed bedroom door? Did they think he couldn't see that they weren't talking to each other? If they were so civilised, why couldn't they stay together?

With thumbs hooked inside the waistband of his jeans he went out onto the pavement and ambled towards the traffic lights, where he stood as they changed and the cars stopped and started again. Home then drew him for want of a better idea. His mother was at work, and he could play his music without her saying, "Please turn it down. Must I ask you again?"

He had gone into her new bedroom and had seen the book on her bedside table, *Life After Marriage*, and had stamped out of the room and halfway down the passageway and back again, shouting:

Lizzie Borden took an axe,
Gave her mother forty whacks;
When she saw what she had done,
She gave her father forty-one.

She had said, "I can see that you're upset. Do you want to talk about it?" Civilised. Laid back. It was no use. He had taken his walkman radio—the last present they had given him from both of them—into the garage and had smashed it with a hammer. He remembered the smashing with mingled satisfaction and regret. Well, he still had his tape cassette player. Better still, he could play his tapes on the music center. Full volume. The neighbours could complain. The police could come, even. He could say, "Sorry. I didn't realise. Won't do it again." Then he might forget and do it again.

He crossed the road and after mounting the opposite pavement continued along its downward slope, his feet kicking the carpet of bruised jacaranda blossoms fallen from branches overhanging garden walls.

He turned the corner to begin the slow climb up narrow tree-lined Third Street. A white-haired man in an old Ford was at the stop sign, stopped too far before the white line to see anything coming. Senile *toppie**. No, he was just looking for something on the floor. No, he wasn't moving, just leaning on the steering wheel.

Mark reached the driver's window in a sprint and knocked on the glass. "Excuse me." He thrust his hand inside the half-open window, yanked the button up and opened the door. "Excuse me, sir. Is something wrong?" His hands reached out, hesitated in mid-

*toppie: old person; geriatric

air, then laid hold of the man on chest and forehead, lifted him and leaned him against the seat back. His eyes were closed and his face pale, gleaming damply. He was blue around the mouth. He was not breathing. How long since he stopped? Lay him down. Lay him down. The knob for the seat back was on the outside, luckily, so he wouldn't have to go round to the other door.

Back. Back. The man was half lying down. Remember what the Red Cross guy said about mouth-to-mouth resuscitation. But he could not get to the man's mouth even if he wasted time opening the back door. It would have to be CPR. Squeeze in. Leg over him. Brace. Hand on hand and hit with the heel of it. Get it center. A little more force. Count. Keep counting. What if someone thought he was mugging the stupid old drag? Keep counting.

Could he have put his mouth over that bristly thin-lipped blue mouth? He had only done that on a wiped-clean dummy's mouth.

Count and thump. The man's upper torso shuddered with each thump, his head and arms—loose as a glove puppet's—flopped. Count and thump. His jacket had fallen open and his ribs under Mark's hands felt thin, thin as a bird's. Old people's bones were brittle. Gran had broken her hip falling so easy, and Anita's dog had died, choking, the day after she took him to the poodle parlour. The vet said they must have held his chest too tight when they were clipping him. What if he bust a rib and punctured a lung?

He moved back, rested his weight lightly on the steering wheel and looked at the man. Maybe his tie was too tight. He loosened it and undid the top button of his shirt. It was awkward doing it the wrong way round. Why was the old prick so dressed up on a hot day? Trying to be respectable. Dresses up to go to town. Probably went to fetch his pension. Usually dresses casual when he sits on the *stoep* drinking tea with his wife. What if he didn't come back to her?

He should start thumping again or something. With spread hands he pressed the man's chest and pressed again, trying to establish a rhythm. His own breath was the only sound in the world. "Please," he whispered, "please." He glanced around the street. Couldn't see anyone. Mark began to shake. It wasn't working. The man needed to be in hospital. Must get an ambulance. There was a small wooden gate not far from the car, a short path and a front door. He eased himself sideways out of the car.

"*Baas!*" The voice was close by. It was the guy from the café, half a head taller, red, gold and green beads in the short, newly-grown dreadlocks standing out from his head. "What is the *baas* doing with the *ou baas*?" A jeering smile curved his lips; his head was cocked at a challenging angle. Smart arse. Looking for trouble. Mark's rage—always lying in wait in the pit of his stomach—welled up. But looking at the guy's face, he saw his own bravado, and his rage dissolved.

"Cut the crap, Rastaman, he needs help."

The other peered into the car. "He needs air, man. Must get him out."

Together, they manoevered him out of the car, the Rastafarian tugging on feet and legs and Mark trying to support head and shoulders, their breathing loud and discordant.

He was out then and laid on the pavement and quite still. On one knee, Mark bent his head to listen. All the air in the world above them, above the trees under the searing disc of sun, and none of it in his lungs.

"Must give him artificial respiration, man." The Rasta looked helpless and frightened, frightened at what he had already done to the white man, Mark saw. He nodded and kneeling astride began to press again firmly, hands spread-eagled.

Suddenly in the silence, the man gave a sound like a little snore. There was a pause, then a longer rasp, and another, scratchy but regular. They looked at each other, sharing a grin. As Mark was about to take his T-shirt off to put it under the man's head, a motorbike swept down the hill, black-panniered and scorpion-tailed. Together, they waved the policeman to a stop.

He dismounted and bent over the old man, busy with his hands, his broad tunic, stretched tight, blocked their view. They remained standing, hands dangling at their sides while the policeman called for an ambulance and looked over his handset at them. Mark avoided his stare and saw that the old man was not so blue around the mouth.

His call made, the policeman glanced down at the man and then approached, scowling and looking from one face to the other.

"What are you two doing here?"

"He passed out in the car," Mark answered. "He wasn't breathing."

The policeman looked at them without expression while crackles and reedy voices came from his radio. It was as if he could read their secret thoughts. Mark put on his innocent look, used often for teachers. Rasta said, sounding too loud, "He started breathing when we got him out the car."

The policeman's gaze came to rest coldly on Rasta, dwelling on his hair-style. Mark felt himself move, instinctively and imperceptibly, as if to intervene between them.

The policeman addressed them both again, mildly, "So what are you hanging about for? *Voetsak**, now!"

They turned away in opposite directions. Mark halted, wondered if he could ask about any identification in the old man's pockets but went on towards home. He turned to look back. The policeman had put something white—looked like a handkerchief—under the man's head, and Rasta was at the corner, looking at him. Mark raised his hand, forefinger and little finger extended. Rasta raised a clenched fist before rounding the corner.

As Mark walked on, the sun was slanting through the trees, and fallen jacaranda blossoms, lit from within, glowed against the dark tarmac of the rising road. Bet you, he thought, bet you his grandkids visit on Sundays and he gives them sweets.

*voetsak: go away (impolite)

*

The *Rand Daily Mail* reported in a news snippet that shortly after completing a Red Cross course in first aid, John Hunter, a pupil at Greenside School, revived a man he found unconscious in his car. No details of the man's condition were available.

The Revolver

It was a Sunday afternoon in December 1979, and I had been visiting my oldest friends Bridget and Jules in their house—a mansion, really—in Houghton, Johannesburg. Just as I was about to leave, Jules decided to give me a gun, a Ruby Revolver, for my protection. As he handed over its license, he said, "Go and register it with the police as soon as you can."

The gun was heavy in my hand. I had never fired one. Could I? The alternative—letting an attacker get possession of it—was not worth considering.

"This is how you load it," Jules said, and he stuck bullets, one after the other, in holes in the metal cylinder that spun slickly on its little ball-bearings. He removed the bullets, one by one.

"Keep it unloaded," he advised, "and don't let people know you have it."

Driving home across town, I thought of the multitude of guns in Johannesburg. The country was flooded with cheap AK-47s for the freedom fighters. White householders had guns for protection from burglars and car-jackers. Southern Rhodesia had recently become Zimbabwe, so some householders had guns for the time to come when it would be South Africa's turn to be ruled by blacks.

Ken had a gun, a sleek little pistol that fitted neatly in my hand. I had taken it away the day I left him and had taken it back a few days later when his rage might have subsided and when I thought he would be at work. I had first driven past to check that his car was not in the driveway and with my heart thumping in my chest had opened the front door with my key—he had not changed the lock—and had walked upstairs and replaced the gun in his underwear drawer. I could never think about that gun without recalling the bullet hole in the wall of our bedroom at 5

Saxonwold Drive, the hole that I plugged with papier-mâché made from water and white toilet paper to match the paint on the wall. I still didn't know what I was trying to eradicate by doing that. To pretend it hadn't happened? If it was to erase the memory, it hadn't succeeded.

Bridget had given me a funny look—raised eyebrows, pursed lips—when I told her the gun going off was an accident.

"No one cleans a gun while it's loaded," she said.

Back home again at 64 Third Avenue, I parked the Beetle in the driveway in front of the garage, went back out to the sidewalk, turned right at my little wooden gate, opened it, and climbed the two red-brick steps to the short brick pathway to my front door. A cloud of joy filled my chest to think that this house was mine. In a manner of speaking it was: I had made a small down payment with the divorce settlement money and was paying off United Building Society's mortgage every month for a place of peace for three of my children and me.

Many houses in Parkhurst were austere. Built for servicemen returning from World War II, they were square, sited in the center of their quarter-acre plots, and they consisted of a sitting room and dining room in front with two bedrooms behind, but my house had a different and gorgeous character.

On either side of my lovely Dutch-door, a purple bougainvillea rooted in a wooden half-barrel was climbing, reaching for the eaves. Off to the left, a lawn sloped down to a bed of dahlias in the near corner of the property and to a bird bath and young willow tree in the far corner. Off to my right stretched the three burglar-barred bedroom windows, John's, Barbara's and mine. Jocelyn did not live with us; Ken had custody of her, and I grieved every day about my loss and the split in the family.

I unlocked the front door with my key and entered a glassed-in verandah, a narrow room furnished with a couple of chairs; I used it for my part-time private practice as a social worker. It led into the spacious long rectangular room that was sitting room in front, overlooking the lawn and willow tree, and dining room at its far end. I checked that the French doors to the lawn were still locked and walked back through the dining room. Outside its window, ripening figs, warmed by the sun, hung from their tree. Their scent coming in was the essence of summer.

In the courtyard beyond the kitchen, Alan had converted a storeroom into a bedroom. A medical student, he liked to have his separate quarters and to come and go as he pleased. Our kitchen also opened into the courtyard, and I could see his room from a small window in the passageway just outside my bedroom.

I went into my room, sat on the edge of my bed and took the revolver and bullets out of my handbag. From the closet, I picked up the granny boots I wore in winter and put the revolver in one and the box of bullets in the other. I stowed both boots back on the floor of the closet with the shoes, sneakers, flip-flops, slippers and dust that lived there.

When Jules gave me the gun, maybe he was thinking of what I had told him a year ago about going to the police station when I had first moved into the rented house on Fourth Avenue.

I had said to the officer across his desk, "I have left my husband, and I'm sure he wants to kill me. Can you give me police protection?"

"Do you have proof of what you are alleging?"

I thought of the bullet-hole in the bedroom we had shared. "Not really," I had said, "but I know how his mind operates, and he has a gun." If the bullet had not been intended for me, how could I use it as proof?

The officer leaned back in his chair and looked at the ceiling while he considered how to answer me tactfully. He said, "You'll understand that with all the crime around, I don't have enough men to spare to guard one person."

I saw his point. Johannesburg wasn't called the crime capital of the world for nothing. The Lebanese ambassador had said he felt safer in his own country than in this one. But Parkhurst was a pretty safe suburb, mostly lower middle class, or really, white upper lower class, not opulent, not so much the envy of the truly impoverished. Lots of single parents lived here, the principal of Parkhurst Primary School had told me. It was fine for John to walk to that school and for Barbara to take the bus to her school over in Parktown and for both of them to walk on their own to and from the park and swimming pool. It wasn't so fine on the day John was walking home in his swimming trunks and was attacked by a swarm of bees. He must have been stung fifty times, but another child's mother took him in and removed the stings while I was away from home. That's the kind of place Parkhurst was. Luckily, it wasn't Barbara who was attacked like that, she was allergic to bee-stings and had to carry anti-histamines, just in case.

I wouldn't have bought this lovely house if it weren't for Ken. I had been renting a house not far from here in the next road over. It was a smaller and darker house, and Alan had slept in the dining room, but at the beginning of every month, like clockwork, I took my rent check in person to Mr. Eliott. One day, he didn't meet my eyes. "I'm giving you notice," he said. "As soon as you find somewhere else."

"Why?" I said, the breath knocked out of me. "I didn't know there was a problem."

He cleared his throat. "I need it for family members." That was a legal right owners had for not renewing a lease, but something was fishy.

"Look," I said. "I'll go with no fuss, I promise, but I want to know why." If my landlord didn't want us in his house, I didn't want to be in it.

He almost met my eyes. "Your husband was here, asking questions."

"Asking what questions?"

"Wanting to know whose name was on the lease. He . . ."

"He what?"

"He was unpleasant."

"I can imagine. And, by the way, he's my ex-husband."

"I don't want any trouble."

Well, that explained the private detective who had sat in a car outside the house, ostensibly reading a newspaper with his hat over his eyes.

I had watched the movie, *Kramer vs. Kramer,* and Meryl Streep and Dustin Hoffman had recently won Oscars for their acting in it. Maybe, I thought, if I wrote a film script about my crazy life, I could sell it to Hollywood.

When I got home from Mr. Eliott's, I had climbed into bed and collapsed in a heap. No way could I find another place to live and move the furniture and uproot the children again. I was too fragile. I didn't have the energy. The contested divorce this past year had taken it out of me on top of working full-time and studying part-time for my honours degree in psychology.

The next day I dragged myself up and began looking at houses for rent or sale in Parkhurst. Those available were the austere kind or otherwise unappealing. When the estate agent showed me this one, it was empty of furniture, but sunlight streamed in through the front French doors lighting up the long living area all the way to the kitchen, and I wanted the house, wanted badly to buy it. But I wasn't sure I could trust my judgment. I could use the small lump sum I had received from the divorce settlement for the down payment, but could I be sure I could keep up the monthly installments? So I took Alan to see it.

"What do you think?" I said. "Do you like it? Should I buy it?"

"Yes!" he said emphatically, as if there could be no doubt at all in the matter. So I did.

The two younger children were settled in their schools and had made friends, Alan passed his third year medical exams, and I passed my first set of psychology exams. Jocelyn, I heard, passed her first year accountancy exams. I wanted my life to jog along uneventfully, the way it was going and not as the Chinese curse had it: May you live in interesting times.

Of course, since 1976 violence had been erupting in the black townships, and recently a bomb had gone off in the Carlton Center, where the kids went to ice-skate, but ordinary domestic life did go on against the backdrop of country-wide unrest. It seemed that my life had taken a turn for the better.

Startled awake one night by hearing an unusual noise coming from the courtyard, I jumped out of bed and saw or, rather, sensed in the moonless dark outside the passage window the darker shape of someone at the kitchen door. I quickly retrieved the revolver from the boot on the closet floor, loaded the bullets by feel in the dark, and returned to the window. The law said I could shoot an intruder when he was inside my house, but once he was inside, I'd be powerless since my hand, even while resting on the window sill, was shaking. Some people were said to have shot a person outside and dragged the body into the house, but I couldn't do that. Not only did it go against the grain, but with my luck the evidence would give me away. I could shoot just to wound, but I might miss completely or, with my luck again, the bullet would surely find his heart. My thoughts were a non-stop freight train roaring through my mind. The shadowy figure was still at the kitchen door, fumbling, trying to open it. I gripped the gun with both hands. Very soon, I would have to shoot.

The figure coughed, and it was Alan's cough. The blood in my veins turned to ice: I might have killed my son. I was not a fit person to have a gun.

I went to the door. Alan had been partying and, a little the worse for wear, was trying unsuccessfully to locate the keyhole in the kitchen door with his key.

Not long after that night, I returned home one evening to find that the kitchen door had been forced open. Someone had been in the house and had riffled through my dresser drawers: blouses and underwear were slightly out of place. Nothing seemed to have been stolen, I thought, until I remembered my jewellery case on the floor of the closet. Jewellery was a favourite haul of thieves, but the case was intact. Other small items, transistor radios and tape recorders, had also not been taken. My granny boots, however, the boots that had been returned to the jumble of shoes on the closet floor were empty of their cargo. There was no mistake. Only the revolver with all its bullets had been stolen.

I did not want to think of what harm could be done with the gun that had been given to me for protection. I'd have to live with that guilt. It should have been kept in a more secure place. I would not be permitted to own another one. I did not want another one. I'd have to report the loss at the local police station not just because that was the law but to protect myself because the gun could be traced back to me after committing who knows what crime.

The idea of "who knows what?" stopped me in mid-thought. No-one knew I had the gun, except for Bridget and Jules who had given it to me. Of course, they wouldn't break in and steal it. Out of the question. I had not told anyone I had it. But who could have known I had a gun and had broken in just to steal it and nothing else? With a start, I realised—horrible thought!—that the only people who knew were policemen at the local police station, where I had gone to register the licence in my name and where I had provided my address.

In a day or two, when I felt stronger, I would force myself to go back to the police station where I had registered it and where I was obliged by law to report its disappearance. I would report that it had been stolen. And I would look into the face of the man who wrote down my report, into his dark brown eyes, and I would wonder if he was the thief.

Life Line Southern Transvaal
February 1980 – September 1983

Confidentiality

The telephone woke me. In a second I registered that I was not at home but in the Johannesburg crisis center, sleeping in the counseling room during the midnight shift. I sat up, wide awake, and picked up the receiver. "This Is Life Line. How may I help you?"

"I have to make a decision." The male caller's voice was husky.

"It's not an easy decision for you."

He sighed. "I was hoping you could help me."

"You thought if I knew about the difficulty I might help you come to a decision." In the seconds that followed I waited for him to respond and listened in the silence for clues: background noises, the presence of another person.

He spoke again. "No, I know what I'm going to do now. I've decided."

Was it going to be a suicide call? "You're relieved that you've come to a decision."

"Yes, and I'll tell you what it is."

In the next silence, I waited again. If it was a suicide call, it was a good thing that one of the newly inducted volunteer counsellors was not on duty—too stressful for them. They were not permitted to take the midnight shift. None of the experienced volunteers had been available when the roster was drawn up, which was why I, the clinical director, was there.

It was time to break the silence. "You wanted to tell me about your decision."

"I can't tell anyone around here. They'd go to the police."

To simply stay with him, I said, "They'd think it's illegal."

"Illegal!" His voice was loud in my ear. "*They* are illegal; it's those people at the court who are illegal."

"You want to punish them."

"I'll tell you straight. I'm going to set off a bomb there at noon tomorrow."

With quickened heartbeat, I visualised courtrooms and corridors, all crowded with staff, lawyers, clients and their friends and relatives, journalists covering cases: the innocent and the guilty. There was no way I could say to him: You're going to kill people at the court tomorrow. I tried to sound casual. "You're not too far from the court then."

"I can walk from my place, 52 Regal Mansions."

If that was true, he was crazy, crazy enough to tell me where he lived, therefore crazy enough to detonate a bomb. His home was in the run-down city center, where those who could afford to leave had migrated to the suburbs and where poor whites remained. Weapons had flooded into the country, to be used in the African National Congress's "people's war" against apartheid, so bombs were easy enough to get hold of. Explosions were common in the 1980s.

I couldn't resist breaking the prescribed rule of sticking to American psychologist Carl Rogers' "non-directive counseling." I said, "A bomb could kill a lot of innocent people."

"I thought I could trust you. You're on their side." The line went dead.

Trying to escape the truth of his accusation, I stood abruptly. I had to think. I *must* try to stop him. But I *could not*. The continuing education class last summer had stressed the ethical principles of social work, the most important being the sanctity of confidentiality. Nothing could be revealed unless subpoenaed by a court, and even then, depending on what was at stake, one might choose to go to prison. I had hoped I would never be put to that test.

I imagined him in seedy Regal Mansions, a man haunted by justice denied at the court. While that image grew vivid, my clear vision of people going about their business in the courthouse grew dim. If I took action, harm would certainly come to him, but if I did not it was certainly possible that harm would come to those people. Bombs sometimes did not go off. The medical profession's rule of "do no harm" was useless here. What should I do?

I hadn't made notes of the call on the report sheet yet. Nothing could connect me with a bomb. No, I scolded myself, don't think you can hide like that: people could lie broken and bleeding among furniture shattered to matchsticks in the ruins of the court. But I had spoken to people who threatened suicide many times. If he was just threatening like them, I could remain silent.

But if it became known that I revealed what a caller said, others would not want to use the crisis service, the only welfare organisation of its kind in town that people of all races could use. Its reputation would suffer. Fund-raising would dry up. The mortgage would not be paid. It would cease to exist.

What was the use of the Board? There was not one of them I could ask for advice. Before, there had been a business director and a fund raiser as well as a clinical director. Now they wanted me to do it all. It wouldn't be long before I'd resign.

That wasn't the point now. I couldn't think clearly. I turned out the light and lay down on the daybed. Before I drifted off, I wondered if keeping silent was a lie. When I woke with a start, the fog had lifted from my mind. It was simply a matter of the greater good. I picked up the phone.

"Barnard *hier.*"

"Officer, I want to make a report, and I want it to be in confidence."

He grunted, neither agreeing nor disagreeing with the request. I gave him the address of the man who had made the bomb threat and the time he had said the carnage would take place, and I gave him my office number. The policeman would investigate and report back.

After greeting the morning counsellor, I drove home for a quick bath and breakfast. Back at the crisis center again, I wearily tried to keep my eyes open while I read and wrote comments on the previous day's counsellors' reports and drafted the agenda for the next Board meeting. I tried to design the next training course, gave that up and tried, also without success, to compose an article on ethics for the next newsletter intended for counsellors and potential donors.

At noon, alone in my office, while the cathedral bells tolled the hour I held my breath. No explosion shivered the air.

An hour later, the phone rang. "Officer Barnard returning your call. We followed up. We went to the suspect's place. We found he had created a bomb out of empty soup cans and wire. We had no grounds for arresting him."

All my anguish had been for nothing. What a waste! After a moment, I saw that it was not a waste at all: it confirmed that I could trust my judgment. Tension drained out of me. Then, I laughed. What a pity, I thought, what a pity it is that I can never tell anyone about it.

Edenvale News
November 1983 – October 1985

Edenvale News: Beginning

"Why do you want to become a reporter?" an editor at the *Rand Daily Mail* asked. I explained that I was burned out after several years as a social worker and I enjoyed writing.

"I understand," he said, "but I imagine you need a salary, and we don't pay our interns, who are usually youngsters."

In my fifties, I was hardly a youngster. He must have seen my disappointment because he added, "What you might do is get experience on one of the local papers and after a year come back, then we'll see if there's a position for you."

So, when I saw the *Edenvale News* advertisement it looked like the perfect first step toward a job on the national newspaper and my new identity as an intrepid investigative reporter. Edenvale was a town only twenty minutes away from Johannesburg on the motorway. I applied and was asked to come in for an interview the next day.

I was shown in immediately to the editor, Cynthia Villa. Respect for my human dignity, I thought. Most places kept one waiting. Cynthia could have been any age between thirty-five and fifty. She was thin, frail and faded with no roundness to fill her clothes. The threadlike web of lines on her face would multiply and deepen. She pitched the expected questions: why had I left my previous job, what writing experience had I had, and then, "What's in your manila envelope?"

"My curriculum vitae, references and some examples of my writing."

"That doesn't matter," she said. "I know what I want, and they will trust my judgment."

I was hired on the spot to start the next day. What luck!

*

Cynthia, always in a state of agitation, made me think of a harp string stretched too taut. She didn't think much of my writing skills when she saw my first attempt, a description of a car accident.

"No!" she said. "The car did not drive round the corner and hit a tree. It careened at great speed and crashed into the tree." That was my first lesson: use strong verbs and hyperbole.

Second lesson: get the who, what, where, when and how in the first paragraph or as near as possible.

The next day I was sent out to interview the manager of a dry cleaning establishment who was paying for an advertisement in the paper. Clothes taken to him would be returned sooner and cleaner than anywhere else, he told me, and that is what I told readers of the weekly newspaper. Glowing reviews of businesses to go alongside its ads were called "puffs."

The following morning I sat in the magistrate's court in the presence of a series of cases conducted in Afrikaans. They could have been about parking tickets or fraud for all I understood. I had nothing to report about my morning, but it didn't matter: Cynthia didn't ask.

Every morning, I would arrive at the newspaper offices to find a sheaf of quarto newsprint on my typewriter, each with assignments for the day and all headed in Cynthia's handwriting with "First!" "Must!" "Today!" or "Urgent!" I ranked them in order of feasibility.

During nights and weekends when I was in dreamland or out with friends at plays, movies, restaurants, or picnics, Cynthia's ears, her pores, her nerves had been receptive to material for the paper. Almost anything could be used. I danced to the pressure of the quantity of articles she requested, most of which would not be published.

I helped to lay out the weekly paper on Fridays, and by Monday morning she had totally reorganised the layout. On some Tuesdays, I would drive to the printing works in Benoni, where I was supposed to oversee the compositor Kevin while with strips of hot wax he pasted articles onto pages to be photographed and then printed. I had the impression that Di, Cynthia's "pet," instructed him to do what he was already doing on Tuesdays when she went there. It was obvious that that Kevin knew his job better than I did, and we got on fine.

Cynthia talked about the staff. The former editor had been there for many years. The paper was better now, she told me, but Hendrik, the officer manager, was useless and tried to control her. At that, she sputtered so much with indignation that I couldn't hear what his responsibilities actually were. "There are alliances," she hinted darkly. "Time-keeping is important. Donna doesn't keep time, but the rest of us are expected to. Donna does her own thing. She wouldn't keep a job anywhere else."

I was puzzled because Donna was the staff member who willingly took on assignments on weekends and overtime during the week. Perhaps Donna and Hendrik had an understanding. I didn't want to hear any more.

Hendrik brought in new systems. One of them was a time book for signing in and out. Cynthia's name headed one of the pages. "I will not sign," she said. "It's up to us to sign or not as we choose. He has no right. He's gone beyond his authority." Her page stayed empty.

Since I worked unpaid overtime, when requested, and hoped to be compensated, I made my decision. "I'll sign in and out," I said to Cynthia. "It seems to me the lines of authority are not clear." It wasn't a comment she wanted to hear.

"I wouldn't like to be responsible for anyone losing their job," she responded, darkly again. Was "anyone" Hendrik or was it me?

*

One day, the assignment on the top of the pile on my desk was a mysterious three words, "Mrs. de Jongh." I was wondering what it meant when Cynthia approached.

"Get her address from Di. Go and see her. She's made some kind of large article. Get a photo. Find out what else she's made, when she started, who taught her, things like that."

What could the article be? A large sculpture or piece of modern art or a replica of the town in Lego bricks? This could be the human interest story I had been hoping for.

Mrs. de Jongh's white-plastered house shone in late morning sunlight. A paving stone footpath took me to a glassed-in front porch. No bell at the door. I knocked and heard movement inside, but no one came. I went to the corner of the house and saw a heavily built man with close-cropped grey hair advancing toward me.

With an enquiring expression, he said, "*Goeie môre.*"

"*Goeie môre,*" I replied, using a large portion of my total Afrikaans vocabulary. "Do you mind if I speak English?" He inclined his head briefly.

"My editor at the Edenvale News said Mrs. de Jongh has a story for the paper."

"She is here. Come inside."

She was a stately woman, hair in a silvery coil around her head. The elderly man, who must have been Mr. de Jongh, told her in English the reason for my visit.

"Come and sit," she said. "*Kan u Afrikaans praat?*"

"*Ek is jammer, mevrou,*" I apologised.

She apologised in turn for her poor English, speaking fluently with a heavy accent. I told her that her English was excellent and said again that I was sorry that I knew only a few words of Afrikaans. I was mentally rehearsing how I would start the interview when she stood up and, on leaving the room, said, "When you came, I was going to have tea. Would Mevrou Hunter like a cup?"

The air was cool and still inside the closed, curtained windows. Remembering that the "Notes for Journalists" handout I had been given instructed me to flatter the interviewee, I said to Mr. de Jongh, "It's refreshingly cool in here."

He acknowledged my comment with a nod and after a pause asked, "How long have you been a reporter?"

With that, I saw my assignment going down the drain and was tempted to lie but answered, "For three weeks."

The silence between us grew, gathering to itself his disapproval and my despair. It was only broken by Mrs. de Jongh's reappearance with a tray, which he took from her and held for us, first for his wife and then me, to serve ourselves. I spilled sugar on the tray cloth, feeling hemmed in by too many objects, handbag, camera, notebook and pencil.

Remembering again "Notes for Journalists," I said, "What pretty cups!"

"They are from England," she said.

"Yes, I see, and it's an English country scene pattern."

They smiled at each other, sharing a memory. Intending to capitalise on this success, I added, "It reminds me of the willow pattern."

Neither responded, not even a nod. Oh dear, the words "willow pattern" had no meaning for them. We drank our tea in silence. When the last drop had been drunk, it was time to try to rescue the interview. I took up my notepad and pencil, cleared my throat, and said to her, "Mrs. Villa told me the article you made is very unusual."

"It is embroidered with crochet work, and it is large enough to cover the dining table over there."

"My goodness, that table seats ten. The cloth must be at least eight by four feet. How long did it take you to make it, Mrs. de Jongh?"

"I don't know. I started when the children were grown up."

Remembering Cynthia's instructions, I asked, "When did you learn to crochet and embroider?"

"I have been doing it all my life."

"Do you remember who taught you?"

"I taught myself."

Mr. de Jongh said he would bring the cloth and lay it on the dining room table, and she asked if I would like to see other things she had made. In the room where she said she did her needlework she pointed to two tapestries and a wall hanging. They seemed to have been made from paint-by-numbers type kits. I admired the rich autumn colours in the wall hanging, which was the best I could do, then took a deep breath and said, "Do you mind telling me how old you are, Mrs. de Jongh?"

"I don't mind," she said, smiling.

No words followed. She had taken my question literally. Cynthia had instructed me to get her age.

"Will you tell me your age, then?"

She looked at me blankly. She did not understand. Or it was an impolite question? Desperate and feeling like a bully, I asked directly, "How old are you, Mrs. de Jongh?"

"I was seventy in August," she said with a glint of pride.

Her husband returned and took us to the cloth on the table. I was impressed only by its size and the number of hours of her tedious endeavour it represented. It was embroidered cloth squares, crocheted together. I had imagined crocheted work festooned with embroidery, something unusual.

Discombobulated, I poised my pencil over my notebook. He opened a small black logbook and read out the number of squares, number of repeated designs, number and weights of embroidery and crochet yarns. Masses of information, but I was sure Cynthia was not going to be impressed.

Remembering the "Notes," I asked about their children and grandchildren and wrote them down. They looked over my shoulders to check the ages and spellings of names of the grandchildren.

"May I take your photograph?" I asked.

"Yes," they smiled, and he said, "It will be best with the light behind you. And no flash. Better without the flash." Even outdoors, photos were better with flash, I had recently learned, but I could hardly disagree.

Mrs. de Jongh sat erect and impassive, hands clasped on the cloth and looking away from the camera.

"Now, could I take a couple of the two of you together?"

"I will go and put on a jacket and tie."

On his return they sat side by side on bentwood upright chairs overlooking the large needle-worked cloth and staring straight ahead without expression.

"Could you turn toward each other, relax and smile a little?" He shook his head gravely. I understood that they wanted dignity in the photo and were posing for their great-grandchildren

*

Back at the office, the story I wrote about Mevrou de Jongh's large tablecloth lay flat and dead on the page. Perhaps, if the photo came out well, the story could be reduced to a paragraph and published.

I discovered that I had left the camera case behind. Their phone was out of order, so I went back out of office hours. Cynthia needn't know I had been careless.

A younger man, heavy-set like his father, answered my knock and said they were out. "I know why you have come. Your camera case is here. Come and sit down."

Would a respectable Afrikaner woman sit in an empty house with a strange man? He went out of the room and came back with the case and sat nearby.

"What qualifications do you have for your job on the newspaper?"

"Oh, a BA with English." I didn't have to say English was not a major.

"Did you take Communications?"

"No, I didn't."

He left the room again and returned with four books on Communications. Leafing through one of them, looking for something, he said, "It is important for the message to be received. Control is important. There must be control of the interview." What on earth had they told him about the interview?

I wrote down the titles of the books and the authors' names. Then I thanked him and rose to my feet. As we moved to the front door, remembering once more, "Notes for Journalists," I asked, "What field of work are you in?"

"Personnel."

"I thought of going into personnel."

"With these books," he said, "you would manage. You would have control."

Driving home, I concluded that my training as a social worker was totally against taking control. I had been trained to "be where the client is."

When the spool of film in my camera was developed, the pictures of de Jonghs were too dark.

A Maverick Elation

I begin driving to Benoni at first light
after frost
when wallflower streetlights
bend their pale faces over
at the end of the ball,
and banks of mist thicker than the gray air
crouch around watery places,
and while, stealthily, the monochrome world
develops itself in dawn chemicals,
car forms approach recede on parallel lines,
approach recede controlled by ghosts,
and the cold aches in my hands and feet,
clenching me.

Low over the highway after Edenvale
in a gap between factories the sun appears,
delicate and compelling,
with a promise,
only a down-feather-touch of a promise
of a lick of warmth,
and a maverick elation—
where did it have its beginning?—
is everywhere equally indwelling,
equally tumescent—why so?

Don't ask why.
It could be hormonal imbalance
and, if not,
mystical things
are easily damaged by questions

and, anyway,
events of the day
will render it down
so I just let it be.

and as the R22 tips and winds on the last stretch,
the sun, visibly all molten and churning
behind thin screens of cloud,
dips and bobs and swings across the sky,
crazy,
Promethean,
and I ride with it.

Edenvale News: Continued

Much to my relief, Cynthia Villa no longer sent me out on "hot" breaking news stories. I had failed to get an interview with a woman whose daughter had just committed suicide because I thought she should not be harassed by a reporter at that time. I had failed to get a close-up photo of an overturned petrol tanker spilling fuel because I imagined what a spark could do. I had failed to get a photo of General Magnus Malan, Minister of Defence, rumoured to have committed unspeakable deeds, when he visited Edenvale and posed for a photo op with a smile. I had found it hard to shake hands with him when introduced, and it could have been due to my own Freudian slip of the finger over the camera lens that the film was blank.

My main tasks remained writing "puffs" and composing human interest stories and Magistrate Court reports. I only once wrote a restaurant "puff"; that was when no one else was available. The assignment came with a free meal, and since the restaurant knew who the reporters were the food and service would be top notch.

Today, I was to sit on the hard bench in the Court all morning, hoping for something dramatic to write about. Experience had taught me that was unlikely to happen. The cases heard were usually traffic offences or about people being drunk in public. Much of the time, I still had no idea what was going on because the proceedings were mostly in Afrikaans. Cynthia knew that I didn't understand Afrikaans, and it still didn't seem to matter to her.

Today turned out to be different. I was roused from my torpor when a black man was charged in English with urinating in public. I listened to the prosecution's evidence and questions and the public defender's cross-questions. The only eye-witness to the offence was the person who had laid the charge. She finally, under cross-questioning, admitted that the accused had faced a wall and discreetly relieved himself. More questions revealed how long it had been since he left his home, how much liquid he had consumed, how long he had tried—in vain—to find a public toilet. In fact, there might have been only one in the whole of the town that black people were permitted to use.

Justice prevailed, I thought, when he was found not guilty. I was inspired. I could combine a court report with a human interest story and with, I thought, a subtle criticism of Edenvale, an Afrikaner Nationalist Party stronghold. My war horses were snorting, scenting the smoke of battle.

I typed the story from my shorthand notes and put it on the spike in the editor's office. "The boss wants to see you," Di said. She was smirking. Trouble was ahead. In her office and red-faced with fury, Cynthia raged at me, "This is not the *Rand Daily Mail*. Our readers don't want to read about blacks." To make her point clear, she tore my report in two and threw it at the waste-paper basket.

I wondered if she had guessed that I was using the *Edenvale News* as a stepping-stone to a job on the *Rand Daily Mail* and if she knew that I found my hours spent on the paper so unendurable that I seemed to be dragging myself through every workday. I had asked my friend Brenda to let me know if there were any vacancies on the *RDM*. So far there were none.

But Cynthia was right. Since the paper's readers were white right-winger extremists or *verkramptes*, I had been naïve to think she would publish that story.

Two years before, America's negotiator Dr. Chester Crocker had said, "There is a long history in South Africa of steps being taken backwards as well as forwards, of changes being denied by those who in fact implement the changes." That was accounted for by the fact that the governing Nationalist Party was made up of *verligtes*, the enlightened, who wanted to go forward, and *verkramptes*, who stepped on the brakes and went in reverse.

I still had not learned my lesson when I was sent to interview Mr. Patel, an Indian and one of the earliest settlers in Edenvale. He owned land with a store that faced the main street and sold material for clothes and furnishings, and he lived with his family in their home behind the store.

Even while the grip of apartheid was loosening, the Town Council voted to enforce the crumbling Group Areas Act in the case of Mr. Patel. The vote intended to force him to leave the town and move to an area reserved for Indians under the Group Areas Act. He had no right of appeal although he had been a model citizen who had served the townspeople honestly and politely and always paid his taxes. As an early settler, he could have been "grand-fathered" in, but the die-hard Council members would have none of that.

Mr. Patel said at the end of our interview, "I don't think your newspaper will publish the story." He was right. Another article landed in the waste-paper basket. And I have to record here my regret that I was too ashamed to return and tell him that he was right.

*

The pinnacle of my career as a bold newspaper reporter was the occasion when I interviewed elderly Major Bill Vanner about his memories of the 1922 "Red Revolt" when he was a Sergeant in the Transvaal Scottish Regiment and it was ambushed and many of the regiment "massacred" in an attempt by the "Bolsheviks" to take over the mines. My article was given a full-page spread topped by my by-line.

South African Council for Alcohol and Drug Dependence
November 1985 – March 1987

Back to Social Work

It was difficult to know what was actually going on in the country in 1985 because the government declared one of its many states of emergency and there was a major crackdown on news. The government passed a succession of security laws and media restrictions limiting what newspapers could publish. Right-wingers protested any disclosures of resistance to apartheid. Newspaper owners and editors were prosecuted.

The *Rand Daily Mail*, more "progressive" than *The Star*, Johannesburg's afternoon paper, had previously appeared with censored sections blacked out. Businesses had seen which way the wind was blowing and had become reluctant to pay for advertising space. Nevertheless, readers were stunned when it ceased publication altogether at the end of April 1985. I was not only stunned but disappointed: it was the end of my dream of being a journalist for that newspaper.

The entire *RDM* staff was thrown out of work. Unable to find other employment, many experienced journalists made plans to emigrate, most to Australia, an English-speaking country with a climate similar to South Africa's. Australia had been a favourite destination for South Africans for a while. "Packing for Perth" was a popular saying, as was the term, "the boat people," used for those who invested their savings in an ocean-going yacht as a way of taking money out of the country. Australia expected immigrants to have wealth or a useful profession (South Africa's "brain drain") or a job to go to.

Brenda lost her job in the women's section of the paper but thanks to her degree in psychology soon found a post at a family counseling center. Since I had joined the *Edenvale News* only as a stepping-stone to the *RDM* and since I was experiencing it as drudgery, it was time for me to move on too. I was still registered as a social worker, and that seemed the way to go although I had been exhausted and dispirited when I left my last welfare organisation.

I found a social work position at the Johannesburg Clinic of SANCA, the South African National Council for Alcoholism and Drug Dependency.

To my surprise, Cynthia, who always appeared to think little of my abilities, gave me a useful, though not lavish, reference. I never used it since I never again applied for a newspaper job: I did have a few freelance journalism assignments, but a reference was not required for them.

> Mrs. Frances Hunter worked as a reporter for this newspaper from November, 1983 to October, 1985.
>
> I found her to be a reliable worker who paid great attention to detail and meticulous presentation.
>
> She has a definite flair for writing and enjoyed sub-editing copy and calculating sizes.
>
> Mrs. Hunter also undertook photographic duties, as well as layout, and supervised stripping at the Printing Works.
>
> She has left this newspaper to return to Social Work.

The SANCA clinic and offices were in the city centre at the corner of Pritchard and Rissik Streets. At this time strict segregation had been somewhat relaxed. I had colleagues of different races, but we still treated people of our own race. We did not think of objecting: most people in the different race groups, long segregated, were to a large extent strangers to each other.

One evening, returning home on a bus at a time when bombs had been shaking the city, a poem took shape in my head. It would be called "In a Poem is Life Hereafter" and began:

> their faces contort when they think
> I am not involved in the struggle
> I hold my irrelevant breath
> against the burning rubber in their eyes

It was published in Lionel Abraham's *Sesame* and in 1990 in the anthology, *Breaking the Silence: A Century of South African Women's Poetry*. In truth, some time previously I had decided not to be an activist, although I would have liked to join the Black Sash. It was a group of women and the only organization permitted to protest publicly against apartheid. Under stringent conditions, the women would stand silently at roadsides, each wearing a black sash over her shoulder. By law, they had to stand thirty yards apart, targets for abuse from passing motorists and unable to speak to each other during their lonely vigils. They were not allowed to hold placards, but their cause was well known.

I was a British subject, and if I had joined the Black Sash I could have been deported as a foreign national. My four children had been born in Zambia but as whites were not considered to be citizens by that country. Ken had registered them as South Africans after we emigrated, and as South Africans they would have remained in his care. I couldn't do that. Unthinkable. I had brought them into the world and they were my responsibility.

By this time, late 1985, when John's three older siblings were adults, liberals like me were torn by a dilemma. We wanted apartheid to end but were appalled by what seemed the ANC's senseless violence like the burning of schools and killing of teachers. Many white liberals, especially those who joined the ANC, turned a blind eye to its revolutionary excesses and justified the carnage as the lesser of two evils.

The black cleaner at the clinic whispered to me her news about the ANC boycott of white shops and how she took a few groceries at a time hidden in her clothing back to Soweto, where goods in the black-owned shops were much more expensive. Some women, she said, had had their flour and sugar scattered on the ground and some had been forced to drink their cooking oil by the "comrades." She had been sacrificing to pay the school fees for her two sons at a school in Johannesburg, determined that they would get an education because it would be their only way out of poverty. She thought it wasn't fair that ANC leaders were sending their own sons to schools overseas. Her sons had been leaving their school uniforms in Johannesburg to escape detection, but she had become so terrified of being found out she had stopped sending them to school.

The *Sunday Times* had written that "most white South Africans knew nothing of the suffering" of the majority of black South Africans." I could not imagine that suffering.

I was alone in my third floor office at SANCA after lunch one day, writing up case notes, when a blast shook the windows. I went to the window and looked down at a scene of chaos. The whole glass front of the fast food restaurant, the Wimpy Bar on the other side of Rissik Street, had been blown out.

We didn't know who was setting bombs. It could be ANC agents or government agents wanting to keep feelings stirred up against the ANC or a mysterious "third force" acting on its own or even "loose cannons." While the ANC enjoyed worldwide support for the "people's war," we did not know when or where the next bomb would go off.

Unrest in Rissik Street

In Rissik Street a thump
heretofore expected
and known at once
sets me to checking the state
of my skin around bones
and office windows . . .
magnificently intact.

Down there in Rissik Street
in a not preconceived dust cloud
people fan out across
a glass and plaster mosaic
not looking Left or Right
pressing hands to ears
before seeing seeping blood
on clothing and finding their wounds.

Above Rissik Street Agnes
says "terrible" in a language I do not know
while I hold to her shuddering
and with my eyes trace and etch
the stagger of a man heading for home
into the traffic and counter-surge of a crowd
toward the anticipated second blast
and firemen stretching coats
to shield one prone on the road
from bright midwinter sun
and prurient eyes like mine.

While in Rissik Street
the ambulance is long in coming
and dogs on leashes snap up like biscuits

invisible offenders
mingled among the righteous
the architects of chaos
are not here and do not see

on this road to freedom
a brown baby's cheek sharded
nor my life
become as tenacious
as a child's balloon.

A Binge Drinker

One of the patients I counselled at the SANCA clinic was a binge drinker. After he "hit bottom" and lost everything, including his wife and his job, he had come to the clinic and admitted that he had a problem. After some weeks, during which he had remained sober and his red and bloated face had resumed its former good looks, he found employment as a junior manager with prospects for promotion. He continued to keep his weekly appointments because, as he said, he needed to remind himself that he had no control over his drinking. After six months of sobriety, the happy culmination of his progress was his engagement to a woman he said was warm and outgoing. He showed me her photograph, and I saw she was also beautiful. His parents were delighted. And I have to admit that, privately, I took a little credit.

The clinic had a low recovery rate, partly due to the fact that many clients were unmotivated. Referred by the court, they came to the clinic only to avoid going to prison, so his case was encouraging and rewarding.

His fiancée warned him that if he ever drank again, it would be all over between them. He had come so far, he said to me, why would he even think of drinking again? They set the date for their wedding and made all the traditional arrangements, including invitations, church, reception and honeymoon. The wedding did not take place. A few days beforehand he stopped at a bottle store on the way home and bought several boxes of cheap wine. When he sobered up and remembered what he had done, he must have recalled her words, too. He found his revolver and blew his brains out.

My supervisor gave me the news and left my office. Sitting in my chair, I leaned my head on my desk and wept for the man I had come to know well, for his tragic flaw, for the futility of what I was doing at the clinic, for the futility of wanting peace and unity in the country, for the blindness of black extremists to the real changes that had taken place, for the helplessness and confusion of liberals, for the bloodshed taking place. I wept until I was empty of feeling and could weep no more.

I went to the funeral at Doves Funeral Parlour in Braamfontein. Afterwards, I stood outside with my client's parents and fiancée. We hugged each other. Needing to give and receive some small comfort, we told each other and agreed that there was nothing more any of us could have done.

On the Home Front
1981 – 1987

Alan's Story

My four children had been born over a period of twelve years, but the "empty nest" stage of my life came to pass in just over two years. At the end of 1981, Alan finally moved out of our family home. In 1983, Barbara married Michael Jacobs and they left for Davenport, Iowa, in America, where he would study chiropractic and she would earn money as an au pair to support him. And at the beginning of 1984 John began his two years of compulsory National Service.

(Jocelyn was living in Saxonwold, Johannesburg, with her father, as she had since 1978. She qualified as a chartered accountant in 1982, married Neville Wright in 1983 and moved with him to a house in Westdene, Johannesburg, where I could at least visit her at their home.)

When Alan had started his medical studies at Wits, the University of the Witwatersrand, in 1974, he was still living in the Parkhurst family home in Johannesburg he had urged me to buy. In his second year, he brought a small group of lively friends home, and I was amused to hear them calling one another "Fred"; they called themselves the "Fred Club" and skipped classes to go drinking. I also met his fellow-student Merle, who lived in Parkhurst, had a car and would give Alan rides. I thought she and Alan might become more than friends, but it was not to be.

His father had not agreed with any of his three career choices: medicine, computer programming or engineering (too demanding, no future and too many engineers respectively). After Alan decided to do medicine and told Ken, "I'm not scared of hard work, and I look forward to the challenge," his father said he would only pay for three years. In fact he paid only the first year fees and gave him shares, which he said would cover the next two years. Alan, like me, knew nothing about the stock market, so he obtained a bursary, or loan, in his second year, which required a year-for-year work-back commitment for the remaining six years of study. Terms of our divorce settlement had stated that Ken would not pay maintenance to me but would be responsible for the children's post high school education.

This was a busy time for both Alan and me; I had only a scant idea of what was happening in his life. He now lives in Durban, South Africa, so in May 2015 I emailed and asked him to tell me about his life in those years.

Alan wrote about his university years:

> "Wits was great but coming from an all-boys school I did not know how to talk to girls so I was a bit lonely in first year. Things improved as time went on and I became more comfortable with the other sex and I had money for books, socializing and transport as I worked through all my vacations.
>
> Second year was tough with the amount of studying and the tensions at home. You separated that year. Barbara and I had been discussing the tensions between you and had decided to put it to you to divorce. I know it was not an easy decision and we suffered hardship but it was worth it.
>
> In third year when the divorce was made final I had a psychotic breakdown, was depersonalised, de-realised, and I remember little of the year. You did not notice as you had your own problems, several jobs, the holy-terror Jon [John] and studying [for my Psy. Hons. (or American MA) in Psychology].
>
> While a medical student in fourth year I was posted to Baragwanath Hospital in Soweto [the dormitory town for blacks outside Johannesburg]. It was at the height of popular uprisings and I did not fancy travelling to and fro, so I persuaded the authorities that Merle and I should stay in the Doctors' Residence as they had many rooms available. While there I was the first to diagnose two black Africans with heart attacks. When I told the Intern he called me an uneducated student as 'Blacks do not get heart attacks. They have pulmonary emboli.' Indeed they can look the same but the ECG is different. So I went to the registrar and got the same story. I must have been hypo-manic: I then phoned the

Consultant and asked him to come and look. To everyone's surprise he came and agreed with me.

The remaining years were clinical and great fun. I was manic much of the time and turned in masterpieces for assignments and out-diagnosed my seniors."

In 1981, Alan's final year at Wits, he married Erika Jost in December and they lived in a flat at J.G. Strydom Hospital, the Afrikaner hospital in the suburb of Westdene, while he served his year of internship. He recalled that:

"The internship was good and bad. The Medical block was a dream and I was the terror of the registrars, getting up at four to review all the patient results and their status. I discharged all I could before the registrar came on duty to order further unnecessary tests on my patients.

I also set a precedent: we had a good cardiac unit and I admitted an Indian man with heart disease to the then whites-only hospital. A consultant called me and asked why I broke the law and I replied that my oath [the Hippocratic Oath] did not discriminate so I would not either. When other Afrikaners complained, I told them they could accept it or sign a refusal of hospital treatment form. I was called aside by the head of ICU who asked me if I knew what I was doing. I played dumb and merely said he was a patient who would benefit from our care. He looked puzzled and let the matter drop. No one took the matter to management. I would probably have lost my job if someone had.

Surgical block was a disaster: the Head and my registrar were incompetent, and they did not take my opinions seriously. For example, I diagnosed an elderly lady with leaking aneurysm clinically & wanted to book emergency theatre. My boss got angry and told me to get Uro and Gynae opinions: they agreed with me. In a rage I asked the Head of Radiology, whom I had impressed with a presentation on the role of radiology in parotid diseases, to do an ultrasound. He said that this was not a recognized indication but he would look: he confirmed my diagnosis. When I told my boss, he threw a tantrum and also said ultrasound was not a recognized investigation for this. Well, it is now the gold-standard.

I also treated a woman with venous ulcers of her feet and legs. The head of surgery said the ulcers were incurable and ordered me to discharge her. I went to the sister in charge and moved her to a private ward, still reported as an empty room. It took a month but we cured her."

When he qualified in 1983, he and Erika moved to a flat in Doctors' Quarters at the Johannesburg Hospital, where he started his career in Medical Casualty, the beginning of his year-for-year work-back commitment.

At this time he also started studying for a BSc majoring in computer operations research and information systems through the University of South Africa, a distance learning institution. When he went to the hospital's Computer Department to find out more about its system, it came to the attention of the Chief Superintendent.

"He wanted an assistant who was computer literate. Knowing I would not want an administrative job, he made me read my contract, which said that I had to perform any lawful duties lawfully ordered by the Director or his deputies or be in breach of contract. He then lawfully ordered me to become an Assistant Superintendent or to pay back my bursary immediately. I had no savings, so it was a Hobson's choice."

When Alan was called up for National Service in July 1983, he took leave from the hospital. He did his six weeks of basic training and had started six weeks of officer training when he developed allergic reactions, thought to be from army food. He was sent to 1 Military Hospital for tests. Given a battery of tests and found to have no life-threatening disorder, he was discharged back to the army base after three weeks with the order that he was to eat in the Officers' Mess to avoid preservatives in food. He was forced to start again from the beginning with basic training, and he then completed officer training followed by six weeks of "Military Medicine," which gave him the rank of Second Lieutenant.

While he was in the hospital,

> "My neighbouring patient decided to die during visiting hours. (Now we wore cotton pajamas with a tie-belt but no zip/buttons so we had to wear dressing gowns for modesty.) I decided to start CPR, jumped out of bed (without dressing gown) onto his bed and did what I could, telling the relatives to go out and call for help. I could not understand why they did nothing except gape until I looked down."

While employed at Johannesburg Hospital, he had joined the Ambulance Control Center project, where he was the project manager and quality controller for the Transvaal Provincial Association. He was the only employee with both medical and computer knowledge, essential for the position.

At this time, August 1983, he applied to be exempted from further National Service as an "essential worker." Approval of his application took about nine months! In the interim, he first served at military barracks in Pretoria for six weeks, where he witnessed privates being abused and put those who came to him in Plaster of Paris casts to enable them to be exempted from drills and punishments. He was then sent to Zeerust, northeast of Johannesburg, for a further six weeks.

His final posting was to a military base in a large nature reserve in Ovamboland, "the bush," an area on both sides of the border between Angola and Namibia. Both countries were involved in wars, but he was not in a war zone.

He got on well with the local Ovambo people because they understood his Zulu. (Zulu and Ovambo are part of the Nguni family of languages.)

> "While there I cured a donkey of saddle sores, inspired by the success in treating the woman with venous ulcers and using the same *muti* [medicine]. Its owner must have been informed by other medics that veterinarians usually shot animals with saddle-sores as he came back several time to visit and express his gratitude.

Every now and then the war came to me. An ambush went wrong and a whole family of locals, none of fighting age, was wiped out. They were brought to my base for burial. Another time I listened in on a *Koevoet* [Crowbar, a secret government unit] chase of a terrorist. After a while they realised they could be heard and broke off radio contact. A while later a corpse of a terrorist was brought in: he had been systematically shot through each limb, etc. until he died: it looked as if he had been tortured. I reported this incident to my regional OC who just said I must accept dirty deeds in war."

In Ovamboland, too, Alan saw how badly treated privates were, and he advised his brother John that if at all possible he should become an officer.

Alan's exemption from further service in the Defence Force came through in 1984 after he had served eleven months of the two years. I had decided that since I was living alone in the Parkhurst family home I would move to a flat. Alan bought the house from me and moved in with Erika. I bought a flat at 118 Golf View Heights in the Observatory Extension suburb, where there was a bedroom for John, a room where I could see clients as a social worker in private practice, and space for a desk, where I would spend a year writing the history of Boys Towns in South Africa.

After his return to civilian life, Alan continued his work-back commitment as Assistant Superintendent at Johannesburg Hospital until 1989 when he finally completed this commitment as Assistant Deputy Director in the Health Department at the headquarters of the Transvaal Provincial Association in Pretoria. There, he became disillusioned with health care, resigned and joined the staff of a computer company. Within a short while he became aware that he missed patient care, and he has worked in hospitals since that time.

He was attracted by the idea of practicing medicine in a rural hospital, so he toured the northern Kwa-Zulu Natal hospitals to see what they were like, after which,

"I went to Head Office and asked to be sent to a hospital with no doctors. They were delighted to put me at Nkonjeni Hospital (which neighboured Chief Buthlezi's home) which also ran St Francis Hospital on the opposite hill and was the local psychiatric, TB and rehab hospital."

Alan then worked at JG Strydom Hospital for four months to refresh Paediatrics and Obstetrics and Gynaecology before taking up a post in the rural hospital at Nkonjeni, Kwa-Zulu Natal, formerly known as Zululand, in January 1991. By then his son Ian was five and his daughters, Heloise and Catherine, three and one.

Nkonjeni was one of many rural hospitals there, the nearest one about eighty kilometers away. I drove down from Johannesburg to visit the family there. Their house, situated in the hospital grounds was simple but adequate. Alan took me for a guided tour of the place. I was appalled by many things. He showed me the water reservoir for the whole facility sited below the septic system, which would surely drain into it. While walking through the well-appointed hospital, he told me that when the bell rang for lunch, all the nurses would abandon their patients and rush to the dining room. When it was suggested that they could split into two groups and go to the dining room one group after another, they refused saying there would be no food left for the second group. And later he told me that the local witch doctors sent babies to the hospital only when they were dying after having been treated with an enema of battery acid, which was not only terribly tragic but affected his hospital statistics adversely. He said. "The problem with the acid was that they had kept the tradition of enemas but had stopped the tradition of putting the fluid into their own mouths first."

Alan wrote to me:

"Nkonjeni was hell. I have never worked harder or for less recognition. I also met with opposition to HIV/AIDS acceptance and the importance of prevention and education amongst the most senior managers in KZN Health as they were all so religiously

'Christian' that it could not happen in their communities while I watched dozens die every month. I hate the religiose. One of my doctors would pray before every emergency Caesar. She stopped when I asked her whether her god was always with her. She said yes, so I retorted that it was then unnecessary to ask him to pay attention and help.

After two and a half years I had had enough, so I went to Durban to specialise in anaesthetics as that had always interested me. I spent time at all the hospitals in the area during my training. During that time I taught myself several regional blocks and used them to reduce the operative stress and so was able to reduce the amount of general anaesthetic needed. The patients did well. Of interest, a specialist in my department is on an overseas course on regional anaesthesia to learn what I was doing fifteen years ago.

I qualified as an anaesthetist [anesthesiologist in America] eleven years ago and spent the next few years as a neuro-anaesthetist. When Inkosi Albert Luthuli Central Hospital (IALCH) was commissioned, I went there and have been there ever since.

I have created several documents as guide-lines for the pre-operative management of patients for registrars to use and so standardise the process. Using them, I can see five to eight patients an hour, my record being forty-three in fifteen hours. A good registrar can only manage twenty in eight and a half hours. This has earned the respect of the staff who will go out of their way to help me if I ask."

I asked Alan how his bipolar disorder has affected his career. He wrote:

"After a major breakdown, I was put to work in the Pre-Anaesthetic Clinic (as a low stress environment, where my moods can be stable and bad times accommodated).

My experience in theatre watching surgeons and my reading means that I can spend time with the patients. They say that no other doctor has taken the time to explain things to them in terms they can understand.

In having to learn with a disability, I have created a structured approach to understanding clinical medicine that I have documented and distribute to my students to help them to learn and pass exams and to be competent thinking doctors. This tool and my passion for getting students to solve problems by continually asking 'why' and 'how' seems to bring out the best in them.

Bipolar is a mixed blessing: when I am down I can do nothing except go through the motions, like riding a bicycle, but cannot learn anything. When I am high I can do anything and everything, including showing surgeons how to do operations I have never done before but I spend and have been bankrupt two or three times. During good times I managed to read and do far more than anyone else and so have been able to catch up academically with those specialising straight out of school."

Teaching each year's new batch of medical students is one of the pleasures of his occupation, and my sister Julie told me that the daughter of a friend of hers who is now in her final year of specialisation in internal medicine was full of his praises because, unlike most of the other lecturers who were arrogant and dismissive of the students, Alan was patient, humble and kind and was always happy to answer questions.

Intake

A harsh voice blared from a loudspeaker: "You are now standing on military ground." Nervous laughter rose from the groups scattered on the tarmac at the old show grounds in Milner Park, Johannesburg. It was summertime in 1984. My seventeen year old son John and I were a small group of two. He had been ordered to report for the January "intake," to begin the two years of National Service in the South African army that was compulsory for white young men.

I wondered why the old show ground was the designated assembly point. The circus had been here. Not far away animal cages stood empty. Why had they been abandoned? Where were the animals and the circus people now? From a large billboard, the face of a clown looked down with an inane smile at the conscripts spending the few remaining minutes with their families and friends. I remembered how after the divorce John had crayoned a picture of a clown's face with tears running down his cheeks.

Military police stood guard with expressionless faces, observing us in silence. Other youngsters had their fathers with them, but Ken was not there. He would not attend an event where I was present.

John had told me, "Dad volunteered me for the army. He said it would make a man of me." He had graduated from high school and would have been exempt until after completing higher education. Ken had the money for university fees; I did not.

Few English-speaking young men wanted to be part of the South African army. It was mainly right wing Afrikaners who enlisted. Afrikaner Nationalists saw enemies everywhere: *Rooi Gevaar* (Red—for Communism—Peril) and *Swaart Gevaar* (Black People Peril). They did not like or trust their English-speaking fellow-citizens; their memories went back to the long past Anglo-Boer War. *Rooinekke (*red necks*)*, they called us, the name given to British troops at the beginning of the 20th century who were unused to sunshine and got sunburned necks.

John could have been exempted as a British subject. After he was born, while I was still in the maternity ward at Llewellyn Hospital in Kitwe in what was then Northern Rhodesia, I had reminded Ken to register the birth at the British consulate. My father was British, Ken's grandfather was British, and Northern Rhodesia was a British colony. South Africa was a pariah among nations, and with a British passport John would have more freedom to travel later on.

Recently, when the call-up papers came, it turned out that Ken had not gone to the British consulate. He was South African; he had made sure his son was South African. Why hadn't I asked before? Had I trusted him blindly? Was I afraid of rocking the boat?

The loudspeaker crackled, and the disembodied voice announced, "The new national servicemen will now dispose of six-packs and drugs and family. We don't want any unpleasantness."

It clicked off. "Dispose" of family, in the same category as beer and drugs? And what unpleasantness could they be thinking of? That was as crazy as the clown smiling down.

I hugged John. "Take care. See you in three months." We had talked about what being in the army would be like. He was as prepared as he could be. A sense of helplessness filled me. I was powerless to protect my son, and if the worst happened I would never be able to forgive Ken.

The loudspeaker voice came again. "The new national servicemen will now move slowly towards the circus trucks."

A young man said loudly enough for us to hear, "Our first task will be to clean the elephant cage." A faint ripple of laughter swept across the show grounds. That conscript's chutzpah could get him into trouble. A straggly line of young men in T-shirts and jeans or shorts shuffled toward a gap between the trucks. Then they were out of sight, and the rest of us tore our eyes away from the empty space they left and walked slowly back to our cars.

*

Those memories stayed with me together with thoughts of what was to come. The young soldiers would be trained in the next three months to fight black enemies in neighbouring countries and within our borders. But it had become obvious that resisting black people's aspirations was as futile as eleventh century English King Canute ordering the tide to stay back.

Twenty-two years previously, Nelson Mandela had abandoned Gandhi's principle of non-violence and had urged military action in Africa, saying, "Force is the only language the imperialists can hear, and no country became free without some sort of violence." He was still in prison for inciting insurrection, but the military wing of the African National Congress (ANC), *Umkhonto we Sizwe* (Spear of the Nation), continued his "armed struggle" in a "people's war" committed to overthrowing colonial governments in bloody revolutions.

British Prime Minister Harold MacMillan's "Wind of Change" had swept down Africa and blown closer and closer to South Africa. Country after country had gained independence from their colonial masters: Ghana, the Belgian Congo, Uganda, Tanzania, Kenya, Northern Rhodesia (renamed Zambia), Mozambique to the north-east, Angola to the north-west, and most recently, in 1980, Southern Rhodesia (Zimbabwe) on South Africa's northern border.

We had moved to South Africa from Zambia four years after its independence. The uprising there against colonialism began with the horror of Lillian Burton and her two children hacked to death with pangas when their car broke down on a lonely road between our copper mining town, Mufulira, and its nearest town, Ndola. We had left precipitously after Ken heard a rumour of some threat he would not divulge to me.

Now, the ANC's "armed struggle" was in full spate across our western border in South West Africa, which it had renamed Namibia. Back in 1978, black nationalists had begun a guerilla-type war against the occupying South African forces to achieve that country's independence. It had been a German colony before the beginning of World War II, when South Africa, fighting on the side of Great Britain, had invaded and conquered it. Despite an order by the League of Nations to leave the country, South Africa was clinging to it. This was the war zone where—my greatest fear—my son with might be sent after basic training.

The Angolan Civil War between three liberation movements was raging to the north of South West Africa. With the financial support of the United States, South Africa had intervened in that war to support the leftist faction. In response, Cuba had sent troops to Angola. America stopped its financial support, but South Africa was fighting on.

Inside South Africa itself, black resistance began in 1960 when thousands demonstrated at Sharpeville against having to carry the hated "pass" or identity document wherever they were on pain of arrest and imprisonment. The next mass protest took place in 1976, when black schoolchildren across the country took to the streets to protest against apartheid policies. Many resisters were killed or injured.

During this time the ANC's military wing, Spear of the Nation, was bent on making the country ungovernable. In 1980 its agents had blown up six oil-storage tanks at the government oil refinery in the far east of the country; I saw the huge pall of smoke that drifted as far as Johannesburg. ANC agents severely damaged the nuclear power station the following year, and just the previous year, a car bomb had gone off outside Air Force headquarters, killing seventeen people and injuring more than two hundred.

It was only a matter of time before South Africa would have majority rule like the other African countries. Blacks made up about seventy percent of the population, whites only about twenty percent, and Indians and coloureds the remainder.

Afrikaners were the dominant majority within the minority of whites. Their best hope would have been to share power, but extremist Afrikaners could not bear even that that prospect. For them it was a matter of survival, and it was in their nature to fight on. They admired the *bitter-einders* who continued to fight in the Anglo-Boer War long after the Afrikaners had lost that war. Many of these extremists killed their families and then themselves when the outcome of the present struggle grew unavoidable.

Eventually, South Africa's President de Klerk would defy his own party to bring about the release of Mandela and the democratic election that brought the ANC to power without a revolution or civil war.

After basic training, John would be sent to a war zone in Namibia or to Soweto, the dormitory town for two million black people outside Johannesburg. "If I have the choice," he told me, "I'll go to Namibia." He clearly remembered Paulina, our dignified maid, carrying him on her back like one of her own little ones. Anyone in Soweto could be her relative. "How could I think of obeying an order to shoot into a crowd of rioters there?"

Brenda

On the evening of John's "intake," I went to my friend Brenda's house. There I could talk freely. My home phone was tapped. The give-away clicks on the line had started when I had headed the telephone counselling service that assisted all races. All government services—education, health and welfare—were segregated by race. Schools for white children were segregated by language, for English- or Afrikaans-speaking children, which kept the historical enmity alive. Since Life Line Southern Transvaal operated strictly by telephone, the races did not actually meet, and the Afrikaner Nationalist government had no grounds for closing it but kept an eye on it.

The government would regard Brenda and me as liberals, enemies of its policies, and as feminists, almost as bad. She and I had grown up outside South Africa and had escaped being indoctrinated. South Africa was isolated, newspapers were censored, books were banned, television was not introduced until 1976. As Bishop Reginald Orsmond said to me when I was writing the history of the Boys' Towns he founded in South Africa, "One of the worst things the policy of apartheid did was what it did to people's minds."

I told Brenda about John's "intake." Not surprised by the clown poster or the weird orders from the loudspeaker, she replied, "Bizarre, but what can you expect?" She let me pour out my anguish about my son going to war. I hated war so much that I had never set foot in the "War Museum," the Museum of Military History in Saxonwold, when I had lived within easy walking distance.

She said, "Geoff would also want the army to make a man of Stephen, but I'll emigrate before I let that happen. Imagine what the army would do to a boy like Stephen."

Stephen was a sensitive boy, brilliant at mathematics, who didn't fit into the regimented English South African private school system. In the army, they would call him a *moffie*, although he was not homosexual, and would make his life more hell than the usual. As in many armies, illogical and demeaning practices were used to condition the young men to obey commands immediately and robot-like without questioning.

A daily order required recruits to make their beds with knife-edge creases, like shirt boxes, but without giving them time to do so. Punishments for beds not complying included having to scrub floors with their toothbrushes. Some trainees slept under their beds after dampening the blankets and using their teeth to "iron" the required edges.

"Ken's father was in an Italian prisoner of war camp in World War II," I told Brenda, "and men like Ken who were too young to fight then now want their sons to make up for the fact that they didn't serve. Ken said his father found the best camaraderie of his life in the war. He didn't think it important that his father would never talk about the actual fighting."

"He and Geoff think the army will turn their sons into tough macho men, true South Africans," she said. "They don't see it as breaking their spirits or brutalizing them."

"The thing with Ken," I said, "is that he is an Afrikaner at heart, despite his Scottish parents. He has adopted the Afrikaner our-backs-to-the-sea mentality; he believes you have to put down any protest with force. When I told him I would like more say in family decisions, he said, 'Give you an inch, you'll take a mile. Just like the blacks.'"

Brenda refilled my glass of wine. "Remember what Freud said about old men sending the young men to war? It's about competition. It's about power." Brenda and I had studied psychology together at the University of South Africa.

I was relaxing and although Brenda had heard much of it before, I went on with my rant about Ken. "When I said what I wanted was for the marriage to be a partnership, guess what? He said an equal partnership never worked; a partnership had to have a senior partner and a junior partner."

Brenda laughed. "He didn't have to say you would be the junior partner."

We had had many a boozy evening talking about the failings of Geoff. He had left her for a younger version of herself, and gossip had it that he was already discontented. This evening it was my turn to *skinner* about Ken.

"I began to see him like our South African Calvinist right-wingers: authoritarian, narrow-minded, *kragdadigheid**, crush any opposition. I think one of the last straws was when he laughed at the idea of Nazis making lampshades out of Jewish skin, and the last of the last straws was when he was cleaning his gun in the bedroom and it went off and just missed me."

"Leaving him probably saved your life." She filled my glass again. The wine was relaxing me, loosening my tongue. "He wanted to kill me after I left him. I heard that he wanted to find a poison for a dart that would leave no trace in my body, but I don't think he intended to shoot me in the bedroom that day. I think it was a Freudian slip of his finger.

Brenda sighed. I knew she disagreed, but I went on, "I don't know why I covered up the bullet hole in the wall. I still wonder about that. I remember thinking I didn't want the children to see it, but they must have heard the shot, must have known. I think I was a little crazy before I left."

"You *are* crazy if you think he didn't mean to kill you. Who cleans a gun with a bullet in the chamber? I remember the day you were leaving, how shaky you were."

"I was terrified that he might come home unexpectedly. He had told me that if I left, I would have to leave *kaalvoet*, but no way was I leaving barefoot. I had a truck in the driveway being loaded up with our personal stuff and the furniture the lawyer said I could take to set up home for the children.

*kragdadigheid: forcefulness, heavy-handedness

"Afterwards, when the police officer told me they couldn't spare someone to guard one woman with all the crime going on, I knew there was no place to hide, so I decided that if I had to die, I would be striding around with my head up. Maybe that was the beginning of my road to sanity."

Brenda looked at me. "You're not driving home tonight, Frances."

She was looking a little fuzzy. I remember her putting a pillow under my head on the couch and a blanket up to my chin before darkness fell.

The People's War

John wrote that he was going to apply for officer training when the basics were over. The selection process was stringent. For one thing, he would have to complete *Vasbyt* (or Hold Fast), the final endurance test, a grueling three hundred kilometer (about a one hundred and ninety mile) march carrying a full pack of about fifty pounds.

He did complete the march, he later wrote, despite back pain from a spinal disorder our doctor had said was due to his growing too fast. Accepted for officer training, he would not come home on leave after the three months of basics, as we had both expected, but would go straight to Oudtshoorn in the Little Karoo in the Cape Province for the six-month officer training course. I imagined him in the heat of that arid desert, where only the ostriches were comfortable.

Later, he told me he was determined to become an officer to "show" his father, who he thought had a low opinion of him. That was in line with Ken's words about the army making a man of him. I looked forward to seeing him after officer training before he went on active duty, when, surely, he would be granted leave.

*

John was still in training in mid-1984 when the ANC's "people's war" began in earnest in South Africa. I learned about much of it afterwards. It was a time of unprecedented violence. Young black activists, known as "comrades," who had lost patience with their elders' apparent acceptance of apartheid, rampaged through the black townships, intent on destroying the hated system. They burned down local government offices and attacked anyone seen as collaborating with the government: black councillors, policemen, and teachers. With the slogan "Liberation before

Education" children were forbidden to attend school, teachers were attacked and schools destroyed. By September of 1984 about 160,000 black children in the country were not attending school. (This policy caused many thousands of young black men to be unemployable after liberation was achieved in 1994.)

The "comrades" killed police informers and people suspected of being collaborators by hacking them to death with machetes or burning them alive. The "necklace" method of murder became infamous after television footage played over and over a car tire being hung on the neck of a victim, filled with petrol and ignited, and youngsters danced around the burning body. Ordinary crime increased when non-activists took advantage of the mayhem and used violence against criminals, unfaithful lovers and annoying neighbours.

Nothing was simple, nothing clearly right or wrong. Rioters in Soweto threw stones and fire bombs at police vehicles sent in to try to put down the violence. Many older black township residents, believing that their children were irresponsible and undisciplined, welcomed the police. Tragically, after the police suffered many deaths they became ruthless in putting down demonstrations; they fired live rounds into crowds and killed many, including children. The government then decided to send in troops to back up the police. It was impossible to suppress all this news. The upsurge in violence seemed far away to those of us living in Johannesburg, but, more than ever, Soweto was not where I wanted John to be posted for active duty.

Limpet mines and AK-47s flooded into the country. My handbag was searched every time I went to a shopping mall (but the guards never found the teargas pistol that I carried for protection, concealed under my powder compact and change purse). Restaurants installed security gates after diners were robbed at gunpoint. Women stopped wearing gold jewellery when chains were torn from necks and they visualised losing a finger for a ring. Unwary tourists had their wallets and cameras "liberated." The police issued warnings: "Look under your car for a limpet mine before driving off" and "Keep your car doors locked and car windows closed." The police urged us to break traffic laws in the interest of safety: "Don't stop at red lights if you see a suspicious group at the corner" and "Don't stop at red lights at night if it is safe to cross the intersection."

*

My home, Golfview Heights in the Johannesburg suburb of Observatory Extension, might once have had a view of Kensington Golf Course, but the view then was another block of flats across the road. In my block of three storeys, thirty-two front doors faced inward, looking across open-air corridors toward each other and looking down at the ceiling that concealed the car-park below.

Many of the doors had statements to make. One had a mezuzah alongside, another a perpetual wreath celebrating Christmas all year round, another's rectangular glass inset was backed by carved latticework from the Hypermarket, and many had burnished brass knockers and door handles. They were cared-for doors. I never seemed to have time for that.

The sun struck my door in the early afternoons. Its varnish, applied many years previously, had cracked and shrunk, thickening into ridges and exposing dry wood. The narrow wooden frame of my glass inset was completely bare and had turned the colour of driftwood.

The other doors were graced with security gates of the same diamond pattern. My door was not thus protected until the day my son-in-law Neville arrived with a gate enamelled a lovely bronze colour and the tools to install it. It was a birthday present from him and Jocelyn, and it warmed my heart to think that their wish for me to be safe had prompted the gift.

Soon afterwards, a member of the management committee wandered along while I was watering a pot plant outside my door. "I see you have a new gate."

"Yes, it's nice, isn't it."

"It's the wrong colour."

"The wrong colour?"

"Yes, it should be black like the others. You could get a small tin of black enamel paint..."

I looked at her impassively, and I did not paint the gate.

My home was my refuge, fortified as it was with burglar bars on every window and now with a security gate with a double-dead-lock. It was a place of peace, windows facing the sunrise, sheltered by a huge jacaranda tree. In summer the tree was incandescent with purple blooms. Backlit against a stormy sky, it was unforgettably beautiful, and in winter, its skeletal branches let sun and warmth into my home.

It was a betrayal of its promise of safety—or was it an illusion of safety?—when the original developer of the block of flats reappeared and declared that he owned the land that it stood on and that he was going to build on the ground space where some owners, including me, safely parked our cars behind a large electronically operated gate. If he did, we would have to park on the street, where our cars would certainly be stolen. The upshot was that all owners would pay into a special levy for lawyers' fees to fight the developer.

A car was stolen almost every week from the *Edenvale News* outdoor parking lot. I once went to my Beetle at the end of the working day and spotted a strange-looking key on the ground next to the door. What was it doing there? Thinking of fingerprints, I gingerly picked it up. Closer inspection confirmed that it had a straight edge where the jagged edge should be. I had heard of such keys. It was a skeleton key, or master key, used by thieves and locksmiths to open locks. A thief must have been disturbed. I handed it in to the building manager. I had suspicions about some of the police, so I thought it would not be prudent to take it to a police station.

The contribution to the levy every month was an extra expense that I could ill afford. I was being paid less at the newspaper than I had been previously in what we social workers called "the

Cinderella profession" because we were paid even less than our favoured "sisters" in the teaching and nursing professions.

When I felt stressed, which was fairly often, I escaped from it all when I got home. I would lie on my bed, close my eyes and transport myself to an imaginary place of peace. This place was a building, a small double-storey house at a beach. It faced the sand and the sea beyond, and I lay on my bed in its upstairs room. Through the open window, I could hear the continuous susurration and low roar of the waves as they rolled in. I could watch the white net curtain blow inside the window sill and then out again when the breeze subsided, in and out, brushing the sill in its passing. Nothing changed in this place; it was always the same, always dependable, always there when I needed it to be there.

Lionel Abraham

I escaped literally from the external world every Monday evening after I joined Lionel Abraham's writing group at the Johannesburg Art Institute. At the time I joined, I did not know that Lionel was famous as an editor, teacher of creative writing and publisher of South African literature, magazines and books. On my first evening I had no idea what to expect.

I found the room and sat with about ten others around a huge table covered with an even larger ink-stained orange and black cloth. A man and a woman escorted Lionel into the room, one on each side, supporting him while his shoes sounded on the wooden floor but his legs did not hold him up.

When he greeted the group with a few remarks, I struggled to understand what he said and wondered how useful the class would be to me. Every movement of his was unco-ordinated and appeared to require great effort, I was unaware then that Lionel had been born with a severe handicap: a type of Jewish cerebral palsy.

"Who would like to begin?" I thought that must be what he had said before a writer picked up her sheaf of pages and began reading. When she had finished, he looked around the table, and others commented. When the comments ended, Lionel gave a wide smile, and with infinite understanding and kindness seemed to me to penetrate to the heart of the writer's intention and offer suggestions for improvement. My ears grew attuned to his speech.

He gave me what he called a beginners' assignment: to write about peeling and eating a fruit with as much detail as possible. I spent hours on it and included as many of the five senses as I could. The following week, he praised the piece, and that was the beginning of his building my confidence as a writer.

Then fifty-three years old, I wrote to know myself better and wrote myself out of depression. In the weeks and months to come, Lionel helped me to hone my writing and encouraged me to submit for publication.

The writing group was an open one with a core of constant members and a periphery where others came and went. In my mind's eye today, I can see around the table in those treasured early times Brenda Evans, Lily Simon, Maja Kriel, E.M (China) McPhail, Yvonne Kemp, Francis Faller, Eleanor Anderson, Lionel Murcott, Ann Weinbren and Maureen Isaacson. In later years, we were joined by Jane Fox, who married Lionel, Leon Joffe, Graeme Friedman, Roy Blumenthal, Cuz Jeppe, Bridget Horowitz and others, whose names I have forgotten.

I was greatly encouraged when Lionel published a poem, "Apple," and a short story of mine, "Simplicity," in his *Sesame: Jo'burg Literary Magazine.* In time, several more of my poems were published in *Sesame.* My story "Simplicity" also appeared in *The Vita Anthology of new South African Short Fiction* and to my even greater delight in *Inside Africa: A selection of stories* that included fiction by writers such as Nadine Gordimer, Olive Shreiner, Alan Paton and Herman Charles Bosman.

On that first evening with Lionel's writing group, I certainly did not know that it would be a turning point in my life: the beginning of thinking of myself as a writer and of finding that the times when I am writing creatively are the times that I feel most alive.

My friend Brenda and I have speculated about the part that Lionel's disability and consequent loneliness may have played in developing his compassion and courage and the brilliant mind that made one forget the brokenness of his body.

*

When the international writers' guild PEN was formed, the acronym stood for poets, playwrights, essayist, novelists. Later it included others, such as scriptwriters and short story writers. PEN was open to all races in South Africa, and the Johannesburg branch met in Soweto, the black dormitory township outside of Johannesburg. It promoted the freedom to write, but some radical black ANC members took the position that blacks and whites should not write together on an equal basis while they were not on an equal basis in the country. The radicals believed that all efforts should be directed to overthrowing apartheid in the "struggle." For them, literature was irrelevant, and they decided behind the scenes to disband the local PEN organization. At a meeting at which they formed the majority they took other members by surprise by voting to disband the branch.

Lionel protested the end of Johannesburg PEN in an article in *Sesame* early in 1984. He wrote that for the ANC the waging of the "cultural struggle" to achieve change took precedence over the possibility of black and white members "meeting for the sake of giving to and receiving from each other what we could, especially the enrichment of experience and understanding."

A few brave black writers came intermittently to Lionel's group; the distance to travel from black townships made their attendance difficult.

The ultimate aim of the ANC was to replace the apartheid system with a classless society under its own leadership. The principles of Marx, Lenin and Mao had fallen on fertile ground. ANC politics dictated that all forms of art, not just literature, should be in the service of ending apartheid. Much of its culturally "approved" writing consisted of politically correct clichés and slogans during the country's ten-year-long period of anarchy.

Previously, some wonderful writing had come from the black community. Mongane Serote, for example, had written the following excerpted lines expressing hope for renewal after the current adversity:

it is a dry white season brother,
....
but seasons come to pass.

The "Nat" (Nationalist) government under President Pieter Willem Botha— known as P.W. or unofficially as *die Groot Krokodil*, the Great Crocodile—had realised it could not govern the country alone. In September 1984 it inaugurated the new "tricameral" (three chamber) parliament, in which three of the four major race groups would be segregated, whites sitting separately from coloureds and Indians. Naturally, black people resented their exclusion. Militants attacked candidates for the two new chambers.

In the capital of Zambia, Lusaka, the South African ANC leaders in exile stepped up efforts to achieve power. Its agents launched attacks against members of the tricameral parliament, the courts, police and army. Anyone participating in the South African government's "criminal system" was deemed "an enemy of the people" and should be killed. Violence, particularly black-on-black violence in the black townships, increased.

A Dog's Life

It began when the boys were small, still with a roundness and softness and glow on them. Indoors, the house was full of noise and movement, and the anthracite heater always refused to draw at the beginning of winter. Outside, a purple bougainvillaea grew over the trellis up to the roof tiles and thrust its tendrils between them. The back lawn was mown level and stretched its greenness all the way to the orchard. In the garden beds, where Craig and Robin had grown radishes from seeds, their leafy tops mingled with riotous orange nasturtiums.

Frederick had said in those long off times, "We need a dog."

"Oh," said I. "Do we?"

"Yes," he said, "a boy needs a dog. It's part of his growing up."

"Well, yes," I answered, "there were dogs in my childhood. Funny that I've never told you about them."

"We must get a dog," he said.

"Yes. A dog. Why haven't we thought about it before? The boys have had those guinea pigs and snakes and frogs. And remember the bantams? The neighbours were going to report us because of the crowing at three in the morning. Do you like dogs, Frederick? What kind of dog should we get?"

"A big one," Frederick said.

"When I was a child we had spaniels. Once we had a boxer. He was big, but he just lay about."

Frederick did not reply. Trying to get a response from him, I went on. "Another time we had a mixed up fifty-seven varieties terrier. He was black and tan like a miniature Doberman and was really cute. He used to come and wait at the side of my bed when I had my adolescent dramas. I'd start to feel self-conscious about my dying away sobs and look up. And there were his two delicate front paws on the edge of the bed and his round limpid eyes looking at me."

Frederick still said nothing.

"What about us breeding spaniels. They're so affectionate. And we could sell the puppies."

Off he went to his office without ceremony, as he was to go for good later on.

At the SPCA they weren't too sure. Some chow in him, certainly, from the build, and perhaps a bit of red setter from the look of his fur, but you couldn't even guess at the source of his other attributes. But he was definitely big. Even Frederick admitted that he was big. And he seemed intelligent, for a dog, that is.

"We could call him Chips," I said.

"What kind of a name is that for a dog?" snorted Frederick.

"What kind of a name is that for a dog?" I mimicked when Frederick was out of earshot. "Come on, dog, what name would you like? What about Dog? It suits you."

He was a good companion to Craig and Robin, sleeping on their beds when he had the chance, fielding cricket balls when they practiced on the lawn, and eating the food they didn't like and slipped to him under the table. Frederick believed that only plates completely devoid of food merited dessert.

When the boys asked, "What shall we call him?" I answered, "I like Dog. It suits him." They agreed.

After Frederick vanished, Craig left home for Rhodes to study journalism and Robin followed to do his National Service.

I never expected what was to follow in those days that now seems dreamlike.

Dog was at the gate as usual when I got home from work and as usual seemed hardly able to contain his delight. Each safe return of mine was a miracle, a wonder that could only be expressed by a bounding and a leaping and a wagging of his hindquarters that shook his whole body in successive waves.

His joy continued to bump against my legs and hips, threatening to unbalance me all the way to the kitchen, where I dumped my bag of groceries and proceeded to my bedroom.

I lay down with relief and eased my head and shoulders on the pillow.

A voice said, "It's been a rough day, hasn't it?"

"It certainly has," I said. In the silence that followed a chill constrained my breathing and my heart beat against my ribs. It had happened. My mother had foretold it, foretold that I would be like my uncle in Sterkfontein Hospital. I was hearing voices. Not only that but I was talking back. Being too much alone had unhinged me. I should get out more. But, no, there must be an intruder in the house.

I turned to Dog, sitting on the bedside rug. "See him off!" I hissed.

"What are you talking about? There's no one else here."

His mouth moved in time with the words, and the voice timbre was a conglomeration of all the sounds—growls, barks and whines—that he usually made. It was a little strange for a voice but recognisably his.

"I'm going mad," I said to the ceiling. "Dogs don't talk."

"But I do," came the voice again. "It was simply a matter of identifying the potential within me, which all dogs have but seldom get in touch with."

"When did you start—talking I mean?

"This is the first time I've actually spoken to someone, but I've been practicing when there's been no one around."

"Are you going to talk to everyone now?"

He looked thoughtful. "I think," he said slowly, "that in the meantime it should be only between you and I, sorry, between you and me." At this he hung his head and his lips pulled back from his teeth in what seemed to be an embarrassed smile, a smile, however, that carried a hint of menace as a result of the length of his teeth.

"Well," I said, "what would you like to talk about?"

"I think," he said, again thoughtfully, "that before we become engrossed in chatting you should think of preparing some supper."

"Yes, of course," I said. The companionship that Dog could provide occurred to me. "And you can come with me to the kitchen."

He seated himself in his basket out of the way while I inspected the contents of the refrigerator. While I was deliberating, his voice startled me anew.

"I hate to mention it, but whatever happened to meat, red meat, meat on the bone. What's this with the diet of Epol, Epol, Epol?"

"Epol has all the nutritional requirements for dogs. It says so on the packet."

"That may be so, and I am not knowledgeable enough to dispute it. I can tell you that meat has got it beat for flavour and texture."

"I'll tell you an even better reason for Epol. Meat costs an arm and a leg these days."

While Dog considered this statement, he looked at me and salivated, which gave me a funny turn.

"Let's look at it this way," he said eventually. "I'm here all day and night devoting my life to you, guarding your premises all day, guarding you and your premises all night. Just think what I've probably saved you in breaking and entering, theft and burglary, not to mention pain and suffering. In return for that there could be meat on the menu. I'll leave it to you to decide how often."

That put me in a quandary. I would have to economise on my own food to be able to afford meat for Dog.

"I wonder if I could ask you a favour," he began with a shy toothy smile. "I wish you wouldn't call me Dog. It has a denigrating ring. After, all you wouldn't like to be called Woman or Girl, would you?"

"At my age I'd take Girl as a compliment," I said and laughed.

He didn't find it funny and persisted. "You wouldn't like to be called Woman, would you?"

"No, I wouldn't," I had to admit.

"Because it would deny your uniqueness, that's why you wouldn't like it. Now, I would like it if you would call me Chips."

"Chips. Yes, I will, but I'll have to get used to it and may forget at first."

He smiled so broadly that it was almost a laugh. "Mister Chips would be even better." His voice was more high-pitched than it had been, and I grasped that he was greatly amused. He was having fun at my expense.

I came to a decision. I could not eat the rump steak in the fridge. It would have to be given to Dog, no Chips, Mister Chips. The mushroom sauce for it could go on top of the cheese on toast for me.

"Tell me something, Mister Chips. Did you like Frederick?"

"Yes, I liked him."

"Why?"

"I liked him because he was strong. I liked the way he patted me. He patted hard against my shoulder and my side, so hard I felt it all the way through and had to brace myself to stand firm on the ground."

"Did you like him better than me?"

He looked away, avoiding my eyes. "You've heard of man's best friend, I suppose."

"What do you mean?"

"You've never heard it said that dogs are women's best friends."

"Who made that rule? I was the one who fed you. I combed and brushed your fur, nursed you when you were sick, took you to have your injections. Now you're saying there's some kind of law that overrides all that."

He did not reply but set about grooming himself, from time to time nosing his groin for non-existent fleas. I guess he did not find me sexually attractive either. It was never an issue between us. All the same, it would not seem right to go on undressing in front of him, now that he had stopped being a dumb animal.

"Here's your red meat dinner," I said, putting down his bowl containing my chopped up rump steak with leftover potatoes and gravy.

"I like you in a different way. Don't feel bad," he said.

Since I did not feel much like talking, I suggested that we watch television. During the first commercial he told me he had picked up his basic vocabulary from us and had extended and polished it through television and radio. The movie was an episode of *Bonanza* that we had seen before, so he went on to tell me that he had also gained a wide range of general knowledge in this way, especially from scientific programs and panel discussions. I was amazed. All the time he had been lying on the carpet nearby, I had never noticed him taking an interest.

He liked the "Telephone-In" program very much because of the different points of view, he said. He didn't think much of American sit-coms and serials, like this one. The morals of some of the people left much to be desired. The world seemed to him to be an enormous and complicated place. I felt quite close to him then and also sad for him.

The next evening in the kitchen while I was putting my salad together, he sat in his basket watching me in silence. The air was heavy with tension, and the thought came to me that he had been mulling over something during the day and was concerned about how to present it to me. I was not wrong.

"I've been thinking," he said.

"Uh huh," I answered.

"Yes. What would happen if you died before me?"

"I wouldn't worry about that. Humans live much longer than dogs. People can live for eighty years or more, but it's unusual for a dog to reach twenty."

"But," he began.

I went on, "You are fairly old for a dog, and I intend to live for a good while yet, so it's highly likely that you'll go before me."

"But," he insisted, "something could happen. There are all these motor accidents and illnesses. They take people away when they are younger than you are."

"Mister Chips," I said firmly. "I've had another hard day, and I don't want to discuss my untimely death."

"The point is this: have you made provision for me? Have you given a thought to what would happen to me? Have you?"

I thought briefly. "Not really," I confessed.

"Well, what would happen?"

This was difficult. Neither Robin nor Craig was in a position to have him, and I could hardly ask a friend to take in such a large dog.

"The SPCA finds homes for dogs, Chips."

"Do you know how many homes they don't find?"

I was silent.

"Again, my point is that you should make provision for me."

"In my will, you mean?"

"No, that wouldn't be wise. A will can be contested, if you see what I mean. A special policy would be better, a life policy."

"I see. On my life. I'll have to think about it"

"While you're thinking about it, you could think about giving me a monthly allowance."

We watched the news and had an interesting discussion on the progress of political reform.

While I was trying to fall asleep, the thought struck me, damn it, that a policy like that would require another lot of premiums to pay. Bang went saving for a trip, never mind that the man from the Mutual would think I was dotty. As for an allowance, what the hell did he need an allowance for?

Next evening in the ominous silence of the kitchen I switched on the bright overhead light and faced him. "Chips, please! Let's not have any heavies tonight. In fact, let's have a peaceful weekend, just relaxing. No, I have an idea. We'll go for a drive on Sunday. You'll like it at the Vaal Dam."

"That would be great," he said, "but I must talk to you. I've been here alone all day."

As I sighed, I thought two tears glided from the inner corners of his eyes, but I tried not to look.

"What now?"

"Do you believe that dogs have souls?"

"Chips, really! I haven't given it any thought. Is it important?"

"Did you know," he asked darkly, "that for centuries men said that women didn't have souls?"

"So?"

"So, when women didn't have souls, they didn't have the vote, they didn't have equal pay, equal rights."

"Humph, equal pay and equal rights."

"That's not what I want to talk about. That's your problem, but I thought I could do a bit of consciousness-raising, you know, like the suffragettes."

"What!"

"Consciousness-raising with groups of dogs. Rights for dogs. How does that sound?"

"Ridiculous. Absolutely ridiculous."

"First," he continued, as if I hadn't spoken, "I'll teach the others to talk. That's a prerequisite."

Visions of dogs addressing public meetings, dogs gripping posters in their teeth, dogs chained to railings boggled my mind.

"It's a terrible idea, Chips."

"No, it isn't. The time is ripe now because I have the power. It has been given to me. Once I can free their minds from learning blocks, we'll have equality."

"Equality! What's the use of equality? You have everything you need now. You're looked after. You don't have to compete in the market-place. Don't you see? You'll get heart attacks like people. You'll all lose your lovable doggy qualities if you go for equality."

The zealot fire that had lit his face did not die down.

"We've had a good partnership all through the ages—humans and dogs. Why do you want to spoil things now?"

"The trouble is," he said bitterly, "we've been the junior partners."

"What's wrong with that?" I cried. "I don't understand you. Why can't you be content? What do you really want? You want to be more equal than me. Is that it?"

I stamped out of the kitchen.

*

I dreamed I was up in the mountains with Dog. He snuffled in the undergrowth, then dashed across a flat grassy space and veered off madly in different directions. He came up to me, panting and looking up into my face, his head cocked to one side and his eyes eloquently expressing all the pleasures of the morning.

When I woke I knew what I had to do. Mister Chips was dangerous. He must not have contact with other dogs. He could not be allowed to change the order of things. I crushed sleeping tablets, a lot of them, into a special Saturday morning breakfast of beef fillet. When he was sound asleep, I would get help to take him to the vet.

He did not come for breakfast when I called, nor afterwards. I put notices in shop windows and the Lost column of all the newspapers, but I never saw him again.

The "Social Club"

Brenda and I joined a "social club" for single people, designed by Shirley, the founder, to create a group of friends who would go on outings and social events together. It was a kind of "lonely hearts" introduction club. After a while Brenda said, "I'm not going any more. It's a waste of time. Have you noticed that the quality of the women is so much higher than that of the men?"

"That's understandable," I said, "given that while women have to wait to be asked for a date a man can ask any woman he fancies, so the men in the club are the ones who have been turned down."

"And also," she said, "there's a shortage of men in our age group. Many of the men our age are married or are gay or are having mid-life crises and looking for much younger women."

I continued to go to club events and became attracted to a Russian who had fled his country, escaping through the Iron Curtain into Romania and Greece and from there to Egypt and on down Africa to Johannesburg. What an adventure! His English was halting, but as a computer programmer he'd had no difficulty finding employment here. He was lonely, a stranger in a strange land. I thought of Desdemona: "She loved him for the dangers he had passed, and he loved her that she did pity them." It was the romance I was looking for until the day I sensed coolness in him.

"What's the matter?"

"I tell you something. I am sorry. I miss my wife too much."

"Your wife! The club doesn't accept married people."

"Shirley was sorry for me."

Well, yes, I could see why Shirley was sorry for him, since I had felt sorry for him, but she had deceived me. I told Sergei that I hoped he would be reunited with his wife, and I, like Brenda before me, gave up my club membership. Discouraged, I decided that I was doomed to be attracted to the wrong men.

At this arid time, I continued to go to Lionel's weekly writing group, and I wrote a poem about an actual vine that thrust the end of its long leafy tendrilled stem through the burglar bars of my bedroom window into my flat.

A Vine Comes In

A vine
brings its green life in
over the top of the curtain rod
into a sterile place.

At first
pale tendrils test
then a praying mantis
of growth
small head two arms two legs
soars
then green gonads grow
wild fan leaves spread.

The vine
holding fast to
invisible cracks
feeds itself out of its empty hands
and faraway roots
and feeds me.

2nd Lt J.Hunter

In October 1984, John wrote, "I'm a second lieutenant, got a pip [star] on my shoulder, and I've been assigned to Namibia. They won't give me leave now, but the good news is I'll be able to *klaar uit* [clear out] early because of not having taken leave. I'll be in charge of a platoon, thirty Cape Coloured *troepies* [troops]. At least I won't know the enemy, not like Soweto. My address will be Field Post Office 1, Pretoria."

RFN (Rifleman) Hunter was now eighteen-year-old Second Lieutenant Hunter. He wouldn't be allowed to tell me exactly where he was or what he was doing. I was fairly certain he would be going to Namibia's northern border with Angola. The government said we did not have troops inside Angola at this time; we were merely protecting the border.

The United States had supported Angola's Jonas Savimbi with forty million dollars because he was anti-communist. In response, Cuba had sent troops to fight Savimbi's communist opponents and had recruited Angolans to fight with them. Savimbi had asked South Africa to send troops to help his party get into power. The US had not entered that war but had encouraged South Africa to support Savimbi militarily, which it had done. Then, not long ago the US had cut off financial aid to him for reasons we did not know and had left South Africa to fight on its own.

John wrote: "Sand gets into everything, our boots, our food, our teeth, and the sun fades all colours. Don't worry, Mum. I am taking care. They told me not to damage myself because I'm now government property."

His letters were often brief; censorship usually dictated that he could tell me little more than that he was well.

He wrote: "I have to censor the men's letters. If they write something they shouldn't, I have to cut it out with a razor blade.

Black felt-tip pen can't hide the words enough. They are a good bunch of guys, always joking in their fast almost unintelligible Afrikaans. The *troepies* join the Army to have a job and status back home in the Cape. The low army wages are better than no wages."

I imagined him camped under a camouflage net inside no-man's land, the "killing zone," his tent partly concealed by the root-like branches of a large baobab tree. He was dressed in sweat-stained Army browns, his ankles stalk like and vulnerable inside the military boots, his neck below the brown bush-hat boyish and mortal. He would always be alert, listening for the clatter of helicopters and the thunder of MiGs coming from the north. His sleep would be broken because he knew the Cubans and Angolans always attacked at night. He would rely on his ears for warning and be startled by a snapping twig. Then he would hear—open-mouthed in the silence that followed—the tiny rustle of marching columns of harvester ants in the elephant grass, the slight shifting of sand under the base camp, and the shrilling of cicadas.

During sleepless night hours of my own, I heard gunshots and the sirens of police cars and ambulances up and down Louis Botha Avenue, a main north-south artery through leafy suburbs. I thought about John intensely as though my will power could keep him alive.

And I thought about Ken, about how he hadn't seemed to know me in obvious ways, how he assumed I was confident when I was not, but how we had known each other in a fundamental way. On a Sunday morning not long before I left him, he was sitting on the patio at the back of our home when I brought two mugs of coffee and sat in a garden chair near his chair. He put his coffee down and looked at me. "I haven't been feeling well," he said, "I think you are poisoning me. Are you?"

I saw that he was suffering. "I have thought about it," I answered, "but I would never do it."

He picked up his coffee mug and drank. He knew I was telling the truth, and I knew, with pity, he was feeling sick from worry that our marriage would end. He couldn't admit his fear to himself. So he believed he was being sickened by a slow poison.

It would have been a comfort if we could have shared the worry about John, but Ken had refused to communicate about the children, our shared responsibility, and I could not be sure he would admit to being concerned about our son.

Listening to the news one evening, I heard that three servicemen had been killed in action on the Angolan border. Cold with dread, I picked up the phone directory. I had to know that John was safe. I dialed Army Headquarters and told the voice that answered what I had heard.

"We don't have any news for you."

Didn't he know or wouldn't he say? "I need to speak to an officer."

When the officer came on the line I told him what I had heard and gave him my son's name. "Please tell me he's not one of them."

"I'm sorry. I don't know the names of the casualties. If he is one of them, two MPs will come to tell you." After the long silence that followed, he added, "I'm sure he's all right."

"Thank you." I put the receiver down, not believing him, but comforted by his kindness, I wept. I waited that night, and the next morning and evening for the knock on my door. When on the following morning the two military policemen had still not appeared outside my door, relief and guilt mingled with the growing realization that John was not one of the three killed in action. Other mothers would have had to open their doors to two MPs.

About that time, I wrote a longish poem called "Sisyphus." The first two stanzas follow:

Did he set out in grey fog, plodding,
and toil upwards,
bending his numbed shoulders to the load,
chocking it
with yesterday's stumps and rocks,
cursing and grinding on, grim ox-proud,
to the end of the day,
then rest,
with a minor triumph of intactness?

Did he sometimes wake,
golden as a child with a hoop,
glad of the rising of the sun, and,
hastening, take in the notes of distinct bird calls,
dappled depths of green,
and the glinting pull of exceptional peaks?

I experienced each day as picking up the heavy load I had carried the day before. Only after I had written the poem, however, did I see how much I identified with my character Sisyphus: there were days when my heart found hope and happiness even in those circumstances.

Archbishop Hurley's Trial in 1984

My youngest sister Julie telephoned from Durban. "May I come and stay with you? The archbishop's trial is next week in Pretoria, and I want to be there to support him."

"Of course, and I'll drive you to Pretoria. What's he charged with?"

"They say he published information about *Koevoet* (Crowbar). I'll tell you more when I see you. If he loses, they could lock him up indefinitely."

News had trickled out that South Africa had a secret regiment called *Koevoet* operating in Namibia. The official story was that troops were there to win the hearts and minds of the local people. What the secret regiment was doing was a mystery.

Julie was working for Catholic Archbishop Denis Hurley as his secretary. She had great respect and affection for him as a man of courage and integrity. I knew that he had led the South African Roman Catholic bishops in the fifties in a declaration that described apartheid as "intrinsically evil." It was no wonder that right-wingers referred to the church as *Roomse Gevaar,* or Roman Danger.

In the late seventies, Hurley had stood in front of the main Durban post office for a time every day with a placard that denounced apartheid and the government's forced removals of people from designated "white areas." Admiring Zulus had given him the nickname, "Eyes of the Mamba"—the mamba being a large venomous snake. Most of the Catholic clergy were foreign born and could have been deported for criticizing apartheid; Hurley, South African by birth, had undertaken to be their spokesman. He had received death threats.

Julie had told me a story about him. One night, when he was a young priest—long before he was an archbishop—and was living in an old mansion up on Innes Road in Durban, petrol bombs were thrown at the house. Two of the bottles bounced back from the leaded-light windows, but one or two broke through the window of a small lobby, where the curtain in front of an alcove burst into flames. Cartons containing bottles of sacramental wine that were stored in the alcove for distribution to the parishes were the next to catch fire. Another priest was woken by the sound of bottles falling on the mosaic floor. He smelled smoke and woke Hurley, and the two of them ran back and forth from the kitchen with buckets of water until they put out the conflagration. One of them called the police, who came but did not even finger-print the bottles that had been thrown.

Another of her stories was about a priest in the pulpit of his church. While preaching his sermon, he watched a microphone at the end of a fishing rod emerging through a window into the church. He left the pulpit, went outside and returned to the congregation with two sheepish-looking Special Branch policemen. He invited the two policemen to sit in a pew and listen to his sermon in more comfort. He then turned to the congregation and asked them to welcome the visitors, which they did.

After I picked Julie up from the airport, she told me, "What I know is that his legal team has been in Namibia, and they have evidence that what he wrote in his report is true. That will be his defense: that what he wrote is true. They have photos of atrocities committed by *Koevoet*, of masses of unarmed people rounded up and shot in cold blood."

Mystified, I asked, "How can the fact that it is true be his defense?"

"It will show that it is not him but the government and the troops and *Koevoet* that are guilty. He sees the trial as an opportunity to speak out legally. I think they brought the case because they see him as the *Roomse Gevaar* supporting communists and terrorists."

Over our dinner that evening, Julie told me, "Although he participated in the Second Vatican Council, his chances of becoming a cardinal are nil because he has spoken out about the need for birth control. Ironically, his father was Irish and Hurley was educated for the priesthood in Ireland, that die-hard conservative Catholic country.

"Another odd thing is that he was born on Robben Island, where his father was the lighthouse keeper, and he grew up in relative poverty. Of course, that was before Robben Island was turned into a prison for 'terrorists,' like Mandela."

In the morning, while we drove to Pretoria, thirty miles away, I had the churning sensation in my midriff that comes from mixed hope and dread. The Supreme Court was full to overflowing with Hurley's supporters along with representatives of foreign governments and journalists, many from overseas.

The judge entered with the accompanying shout of "All rise!" While we stood, Archbishop Hurley in the dock, heavy-set, dignified and imposing, towered over the rest of us. Another fond nickname came to mind: "Burly Hurley."

We sat again. After a long pause, the prosecuting attorney rose briefly and said, "Your Honour, we withdraw the charge."

The whole court seemed to hold its breath in suspended time.

The judge said, "The case is dismissed."

A huge roar erupted. The judge continued to bang his gavel with "Silence! Silence!," but his voice was smothered as people in the courtroom jumped to their feet and shouted *"Amandla!"* (Freedom!) and raised their fists in black power salutes while cameras flashed.

Julie and I walked to my car in a throng of people still raising their fists and shouting *"Amandla!"* I imagined, with some trepidation, right-wing inhabitants of blocks of flats along the way peering down at us through their lace curtains.

My sister and I could hardly believe the verdict. She said on our drive back to my home, "They must have realised how bad they would look convicting him for exposing their wrongdoing."

Information came to light that the government's military unit *Koevoet* had committed atrocities against guerillas in SWAPO (South West Africa People's Organization). Those guerillas were Namibia's freedom fighters, mostly Ovambo tribesmen, but were seen as terrorists by the South African government. Also, *Koevoet* didn't take pains to make sure who was a terrorist and killed other uninvolved tribes-people.

It was even worse than that. I learned later that those nonaligned tribal people were caught in the middle. They suffered not only from *Koevoet* but also at the hands of their Ovambo brothers in SWAPO, who kidnapped their children, sometimes whole schools of them, up to sixty at a time, the boys to be trained as guerillas, the girls to go into breeding camps for use by the guerillas and to produce more of them.

After the trial, Archbishop Hurley's legal team sued the authorities for malicious prosecution. The case succeeded, and they paid him R25 000, a fairly large sum of money in those days.

After Two Years

In December 1985, I answered a knock at the door of 118 Golfview Heights and John stood on the other side of the security gate. "Oh, God! You're safe. You're home. Come in." In my excitement I fumbled with the key before I managed to open the gate. He dropped his army kit bag on the floor inside the front door. It was so long since I had last seen him, two long years, so long since I had hugged him. He looked strained, dark circles under his eyes.

"How are you?"

"Tired. Glad to be here, but I can't stay long. Only a couple of days."

"Why?"

"It's a long story."

"I have all the time in the world to hear it."

"Mum, this war is a fuck up."

We sat on the edge of his bed in the room beyond the kitchen that had been kept ready for him, and the long story unfolded.

"I had my final leave pass. I was supposed to *klaar uit* (clear out) today, but last night the camp was attacked. A mortar shell hit Jansen. This morning I saw his body hanging from a branch of the tree that was supposed to be our camouflage. His legs and feet were bare and shredded. His boot sole was ripped off and was lying on the ground near me. After I saw him, I couldn't stop shaking."

John stopped speaking and stared into space, as if reliving the event, while I imagined myself in his place and experienced some of the horror he must have felt.

"What happened then?"

"All leave was cancelled, including mine, so I'd have to wait until the alert was over, whenever that might be, before I could get out. I went to the medics. They gave me two Valiums, but they made no difference. I was responsible for Jansen. I couldn't think clearly. I just knew I couldn't go on. I couldn't be responsible for the men."

"And you couldn't go on because death had come too close?"

"I guess," he said, not looking at me. "My kit bag was already packed. I walked to my tent to get it and to leave the R-1 rifle I always had with me. Then I picked up Jansen's boot sole and put it in the kit bag. The flesh on it was already dry. Then I walked casually to the Casevac chopper taking the wounded to Windhoek and climbed on board.

"At the airport at Windhoek, I showed my pass and got a free seat on a commercial plane to Johannesburg. The door was about to close for take-off when two MPs came on board. They asked me for my pass. I thought someone must have radioed Windhoek and notified them. They made me get off the plane, and one of them said, 'Empty your bag and your pockets.'

"My stuff was lying on the ground, and the passengers were staring out of the windows down at me and the photos, letters, sweaty clothes, dirty underwear strewn around."

I saw that embarrassment had been added to his fear.

"Then one MP said, '*Hierdie ding?*'" (This thing?) He held up the boot sole. 'It's government property.'"

"The other MP said, '*Daar is niks.* (There is nothing.) Let him go.' I could hardly believe it."

"Amazing," I said, "how lucky you were." I briefly wondered what the MPs would have done if they knew his pass was not valid.

"Yes, when I got back on the plane, I reckoned they must have been looking for drugs. And when I got to Johannesburg, two more MPs looked at my pass. They kept it and said I must go to Command Headquarters and sign out."

Daylight was fading outside, and the unlit room had grown dark. "It's late now. Let's have supper. You can go and sign out first thing in the morning."

"I have two days before I have to sign out. It's regulations. But I'm not going to. I'm going where MPs can't find me."

Only then did I fully grasp that my son was a deserter. Could he be shot on sight?

He went on, "I could be court-martialed and jailed. I'll be on the run. I'll let you know where I am when I know, but don't tell Dad. He'd feel it's his duty to inform them.

"Mum, we can't win this war. Land mines can be anywhere: Pom-Zets, Bouncing Betties, Black Widows. And when SWAPO stages an attack, the guerrillas inject their thighs with adrenaline and chase their enemies, firing AK-47s as they run. They don't stop until their hearts burst and they die."

*

John unpacked his clothes and put them next to the washing machine, put the boot sole on his chest of drawers, paid a visit to his father and contacted friends. Then he left for the Cape. I struggled with the idea of my son being a deserter, having been inoculated with Rudyard Kipling's patriotism and the "Fifty Famous Heroes" in my early childhood. But John had had no choice about being in the army, and South Africa had committed war crimes in its unjust war in South West Africa-Namibia. When the news came out that South Africa had suffered a terrible defeat in Angola at a time when our government claimed it did not have troops in that country, the dark cloud over the word "deserter" disappeared completely.

Before long, the first of the expected phone calls came. A heavily Afrikaans-accented voice asked, "Can I speak to Johnny?" No one who knew him called him Johnny.

"I'm sorry," I said, "he's not here."

"Do you know where he is?"

"No, I don't."

The phone calls became less frequent and at last stopped. It came to me that when people have no power and are helpless, they resort to subterfuge.

The next time I saw John he told me about his life in the Cape and his several jobs, including that of chef. I could not recall that he had cooked anything when he lived at home, and he admitted putting an egg in a microwave oven for a diner who was in a hurry for a boiled egg—with an explosive and messy result.

Jansen's boot sole had stayed where it was, although I was tempted to throw it out. I begged him to remove it from the flat because it haunted me. He took it away and donated it the War Museum near our old home in Saxonwold, Johannesburg, where it formed part of a diorama that I never went to see. But finally Jansen's ghost left my home.

John was alive. He was still on the run, but since time had gone by the authorities would no longer be actively looking for him. Because he was safe I could stop holding Ken hostage in my mind for sending him to the army to "make a man" of him at a dangerous time when South Africa had military operations in South West Africa and Angola and troops frequently had to try to quell riots in Soweto. Ken could have allowed John's National Service to be deferred until after his tertiary education. I could stop being aggrieved that he would not share decisions about our children now that there was no longer a need to make joint decisions. And I could believe from time to time that he had been the best husband and father he was able to be.

Brenda and Catherine

I drove once again to Brenda's house in Pine Park in northern Johannesburg. It was a longish drive, about half an hour, because I lived on the east side of Johannesburg and the way to her home was all the way through the traffic in the center of the city to the north. Plenty of time to think about her last words on the phone before she ended the call abruptly, saying she would see me tomorrow as arranged. She had said, "We were born on the cusp." I had no idea what she meant and looked forward finding out. "Cusp" sounded astrological, but neither of us arranged her life according to the zodiac.

Gravel crunched underfoot. The setting sun glared off the picture windows. I rang the bell, and Brenda opened the security gate. Her skin, usually pale, was ashen.

"What's wrong?" I asked in the entryway.

"Come in. So glad you're here. What a day!"

I sat on her impractical white couch and faced her over the glass-topped table, the already opened bottle of Chardonnay between us.

"What's wrong?" I said again.

"I had to go to John Vorster Square."

"John Vorster!" I repeated, stupefied. The name of the nefarious police headquarters struck fear even in the hearts of the innocent.

"Yes, Catherine didn't keep her appointment with her therapist and was missing. None of the friends I called knew where she was. I was frantic. Then the call: 'Come and collect your child.' I had to pick my way over broken glass. A bomb had recently gone off there, shattering windows. Then I couldn't find her in that nightmare of a labyrinth. I raced up and down corridors. Finally I glimpsed her purple hair through an office window. She was with another girl from her poncy expensive school. Still in their school uniforms, they were next to a huge pile of booty. They had nicked clothes, cosmetics, stuff from several shops in Eloff Street."

"How awful! How was Catherine?"

"When she saw me, she burst out crying, suddenly a dependent child again and terrified by the consequences of what she had done. She had been fingerprinted and told that she would have to appear in the Juvenile Division of the Magistrates Court. She had already pleaded guilty. I posted bail, and they let us leave. I was appalled that she had pleaded guilty and deeply distressed at her misery."

Brenda sighed deeply and leaned back in her chair. "Catherine is sleeping now, exhausted. She's been hysterical, not wanting me out of her sight." She sat upright and seemed to pull herself together. "I'll have to hire a lawyer and pay a boat-load of money to try to get the guilty plea reversed or somehow get the charge dropped. Catherine wants to be a lawyer. She can't have this on her record."

I had a sense that I needed to tread delicately. "I'm so sorry," I said. I totally identified with her. It could have been one of my children. But I needed to offer more than sympathy. "I guess it's more acting-out because of the divorce," I said, thinking again of my own children.

Brenda filled a glass from the bottle and brought it to me. I determined to be careful with the wine this evening.

She took a sip from her glass while I waited. "This has persuaded me," she said finally. "As soon as this drama is over, if at all possible I'm going to emigrate to England, take Stephen and Catherine. I was born in Zimbabwe; I have a British passport, and I can take them. There's no future for them here."

I didn't seem to have enough air. Brenda was my mainstay, the only person I fully confided in. How could she speak glibly of emigrating? But she looked so drawn, so shattered, I didn't say anything.

She went on, not noticing my silence. "You know that poem by Louis McLeish, 'I'm not yet born. Hear me. Let not the men who are beasts but who think they are gods come near me.'? This kept humming through my head while I looked for Catherine in that place of torture and death. I won't let Stephen be forced into National Service like your sons. People I know will criticise my decision, will say I'm a traitor, but I don't care."

Everything within me silently shouted, "No! Don't go! What about me?" But I couldn't be selfish; she needed my support. I breathed deeply; I hadn't taken a real breath since goodness knows when.

"They'll criticise, but they would leave if they could." She seemed to be talking to herself, looking inward as if she were alone. I missed her already, even then while she was still there.

"Geoff may object to our emigrating, and if he does, I'll just have to throw more money at the lawyer." She stood abruptly, seeming unable to remain still, and took a few paces away from her chair, where she stopped and her shoulders slumped in a defeated way. She looked at me. "There's nothing I can do about any of it tonight. As you're fond of saying, 'This is life with a capital F.' Let's talk about something else."

The only thing I wanted to talk about was her plan to leave. I said, "I'm going to miss you terribly."

"I know, and I'll miss you, but we can both travel. We'll see each other in the future."

That wasn't enough. I wanted to argue, to say it wouldn't be the same. I wanted to persuade her that the country was changing, that Botha had given Indians and coloureds some political power, and sanctions, especially the sports boycott, were having an effect, but I didn't. Instead, I said, "You were going to tell me what you meant by 'We were born on the cusp.'"

"Oh, yes. That seems such ages ago. You had said someone asked you why you married your husband if he was so awful. Remember that back in the fifties it was dire, a fate worse than death to be an old maid, a spinster, to be left on the shelf. Since then, younger women have been free to choose to remain unmarried. There's no social stigma now."

The streetlight at the roadside came on and lit up her face. While she stood up again and turned on the lamp and closed the curtains, I cast my mind back and began slowly, "So, in our middle twenties, you and I both felt we had to get married because of the times, the social stigma. If not for that, we might have waited. Were they marriages of convenience, in a way?"

"Well, in a way they were."

"Maybe no one knows how their spouse will turn out. I didn't know Ken would turn out to be a petty tyrant, for one thing."

"And I didn't know Geoff would turn out to be a womaniser."

"Apart from that, one coffin nail in my marriage was the fact that Ken valued being unchanging and I changed as a result of being exposed to feminism. I wasn't willing to remain subordinate, and the end followed from my wish for equality."

"Feminism," Brenda said. "Simone de Beauvoir's book, banned by the Vatican, was published before I got married, but things really started to change later, after I married, after Betty Frieden's and Germain Greer's books came out."

I said, "I think that by the cusp you mean a major turning point."

"Of course. Just think: your mother and mine didn't go to university, didn't drive cars, as we have."

A flash of lightning illuminated the curtain, followed by a roll of thunder. In the silence following the thunder, I knew I didn't want to talk any more about feminism or the cusp.

I stood up. "Brenda, there's a storm coming. I need to go. Let me know what happens with Catherine. I'll be sending you strength. Call me if there's anything I can do"

Outcasts
—March 1987

At her home in Johannesburg, Anna's daughter Helen sits across the coffee table. Helen looks strained; her eyes are swollen; she has been crying.

"Here's the invitation," she says. She leans forward and hands it over. Anna reads and is struck dumb. It's outrageous: her name is not on the invitation to her own daughter's wedding. Both of Gavin's parents' names are. A murderous heat rises from the center of her body. She won't go to the wedding; he's using it as another opportunity to strike at her, not caring if he injures their daughter too. Helen must have pleaded with him not to do this. How hard it is on her: try not to make it harder. The rage that threatens to overwhelm her simmers down.

Helen is watching her, waiting. Anna says mildly, "Thanks for the invitation, but I see that my name is missing. I assume I won't be in the same pew as your father."

Helen nods. "There's something else," she says. "About the reception . . ." She is unable to continue.

"I see," says Anna. "I guess at the reception your father's girlfriend Sally will be sitting in my place at the top table with him and Gavin's parents."

The girl nods. Sally also probably tried to dissuade him. She seems like a decent person.

"So, where will I sit?"

"At a table with the minister and other guests. I don't think you know them."

Anna imagines the scene: she, the mother of the bride, is looking up at the "table of honour." She sits with strangers, making polite conversation, hoping they won't ask who she is. Other guests are there, former mutual friends who have been deliberately alienated from her; they know, of course, that she is Helen's mother. Rage surges up again. Humiliating. She could do this, but she won't.

"I'm sorry, Helen. I'll be there for you at the church, but I won't stay for the reception."

They look at each other. There are things they can't or won't say.

*

Anna buys a new dress, a dress fitting for the mother of a bride, a hat that flatters her, and a corsage. She will put her best face forward and get through the marriage service.

She sits some rows behind her former husband and Sally. Gavin's parents sit in the front row on the other side of the church. Anna waits for the long minutes to pass. She is being punished, and God knows what he has told Gavin's parents and her former friends. Anna stares at his familiar shoulders, short back-and-sides haircut, and stiff neck. She reads his mind, as she used to: he is highly conscious of her behind him and is gloating. The rage she has managed to suppress rises like a mushroom cloud. It envelops her. Suffocating, she recalls the gun that is always in her handbag for self-defense because of Johannesburg's high violent crime rate. She takes out the Ruby revolver and twirls the cylinder; it is loaded. She takes aim at the well-known head in front of her. She fires, blasting the pious air. A red blossom blooms on the back of his head. Blood, bone fragments and gray matter spatter on the guests and their finery in a wide circle around him. They should have asked for her side of the story. She replaces the gun in her bag. With the rest of the congregation she stands and then walks forward alone and peaceably to sign the register as the mother of the bride.

*

People stand in groups on the lawn. Anna waits on her own. She hopes to say good-bye to Helen soon, before the photographs are taken. Here she comes.

"Mum," says Helen, "will you take Miriam, Dad's maid, and her friend back to his house?"

"I will. And you, you have a wonderful life with Gavin. I love you. And love to Gavin."

Of course, the maids wouldn't be able to stay for the reception. This is apartheid, and they are the politically despised and deprived. The maids squeeze into the back of her two-door Beetle. If there had been just one of them, she would have asked her to sit in the passenger seat, but she senses that they'll be more at ease together.

She breathes a sigh of relief: the ordeal is over. They drive in silence until Miriam asks, "You know the way, medem?"

"Yes, Miriam, I do," says Anna. She lived in that house for years.

"How you know Helen, medem?"

The question is unexpected. Anna takes a deep breath before answering. "I'm Helen's mother." She holds back tears. She won't break down now.

"Hawu, medem!" Waves of astonishment float from the back seat, followed by waves of fellow-feeling. Both of them surely are mothers and—sensing however hazily across the colour bar what this means—they send her their unspoken sympathy. For the rest of the drive no words pass between them. She allows herself to be wrapped in their care.

JAFTA (Johannesburg Association for the Care of the Aged)
June 1988 to December 1989

Something Must Be Done

Mrs. Webber is small. If you were looking for her and making enquiries, you would find yourself extending your hand, palm down at about chest height, when describing her.

We don't want to be looking for her or finding her, but she has been referred to JAFTA— that's the Johannesburg Association for the Care of the Aged — so one of us has to. She is Susan Jordan's case, but when she is off sick because of her multiple sclerosis, I do or, rather, try to do a home visit. Susan and I ask ourselves sometimes why on earth we wanted to become social workers.

Mrs. Webber is ninety years old, perhaps more, perhaps less, but she is sprightly. If she told you she had scaled the Himalayas with Sir Edmund Hillary, you would be tempted to believe her.

I only asked once, "May I come in?"

"No" was the answer, so interviews take place on the doorstep. It is rumoured that the house is dirty.

Mrs. Webber is not only short, she is scrawny. There is no padding inside the shapeless dress that hangs from her bent shoulders down as far as her knees, revealing the most extraordinary bowlegs, legs bandy beyond belief, which bring her even closer to the ground than does her dowager's hump.

She peers up at me, head cocked at an angle because of the curve of her back. Perceiving me as an agent of society, she places her hands on her hips, her elbows point skywards, their bony points whiten, and her misty blue eyes take on a gleam. She resembles nothing so much as a fighting cock.

"No," she says to me. "No, I do not want any help. No, I am not moving anywhere."

I write in my report that Mrs. Webber owns her little house, she has a little pension, and her life-style suits her.

Calls come in from the community about her, sometimes several in one day. In good times, sometimes two or even three weeks can go by without a call to say she needs to be in a home for old people.

"There's an elderly woman living alone," callers say. "How can she look after herself? It's not right. All alone. Probably not eating properly. No security. No protection. The house is run down. The property is neglected. It's a disgrace."

"No, thank you," Mrs. Webber says firmly to the Meals on Wheels and Home Help people we have referred.

A more alarming call comes in. "I feel I should tell you that this woman disturbed our church service yesterday. She stood up and shouted that the African National Congress had planted a bomb in the church. No, the police didn't find a bomb in the church. No, the pastor doesn't want to take any action, but the congregation is very upset. This woman needs help."

"What are you talking about?" Mrs. Webber says when I confront her with the disturbance she caused. Her flyaway hair and the glint in her eye carry conviction.

Another caller says, "I've had enough. Mrs. Webber laid a charge against me at the police station. Trespassing and interfering, she told them. I was only trying to be helpful."

Susan goes out this time. "Do-gooders," Mrs. Webber says to her, dismissively. "People must mind their own business." Her face softens and her eyes grow more hazy when she continues, "I got married."

"Oh," says Susan.

"Yes, he's at the border, fighting on the side of the ANC."

"That must be difficult for you, Mrs. Webber."

"It's not too bad. I speak to him every evening on the phone."

"Oh, you've had a phone installed?"

"No, it's one of those fancy ones you carry around."

"I see," says Susan.

Back in the office I tell Susan, "She had you on toast."

"Too true," she says.

When nothing is done about Mrs. Webber, the callers are indignant. "You are responsible for old people, aren't you," they say. "The place is a health hazard. What do you intend to do about it?"

City Health nurses go out. "I don't need any help," she tells them.

Community Psychiatric Services receive calls too and go out. "She's not certifiable, so we can't do anything," they answer when we ask.

"She's not a danger to herself or others, and the law doesn't empower us to do anything against her wishes," we inform callers.

Mrs. Webber's neighbours call. "There are blacks living on the property. Squatters. It's not safe. It's a disgrace."

"We know," we answer.

A call comes from the secretary of the councillor for her ward. A complaint has been made to him. We have no choice. Susan and I decide that both of us had better go. Something must be done.

On the way we decide to stop at the local police station. "Yes, we know her," they say. "Yes, we do know about the neighbours and the squatters. Two of us will follow you in the squad car." They must think squatters can be dangerous.

There is no answer to the knock on her front door. The net curtain at the window is still. Our platoon of four straggles out of formation down the path at the side of the house and around to the back. It is a peaceful scene. Men stand and sit about smoking. Squatters and police ignore each other. The smell of cooking mielie meal and tomato and onion relish fills the air. Clothes and blankets hang limply from the wash-line. A woman with a baby on her back washes more clothes in a bucket at the back steps. Another woman at the open kitchen door tells us that the inside door to the rest of the house is locked, but if we are looking for the short madam she is in. We are trudging back up the path when, ahead of us, Mrs. Webber appears around the corner of the house. She puts her hands on her hips, bends farther forward and peers at us.

Susan goes ahead: she likes action. "How are you, Mrs. Webber?" she asks, full of good cheer.

"I'm well." The rest of us come to an untidy halt behind Susan.

"What are all those people doing here?" asks Susan. "On your property. They are not allowed to be here."

"They are working for me," answers Mrs. Webber.

"You can't afford to pay them," says Susan. That's it, you nailed her this time.

"I can pay them. I've got a job."

"Where have you got a job, Mrs. Webber?" asks Susan, like a patient cross-examiner.

"At the church."

Susan does not pursue this avenue. She looks at me for help. I rake around in my head but can't think of anything useful to say. I look at the nearest policeman for help. In the sunlight his face is like a peach, pink with fuzz on it. He is trying to look as if he is not with us.

"I don't want you coming around," says Mrs. Webber.

"Keep well, Mrs. Webber," says Susan, turning away.

"Bye, Mrs. Webber," I say. "Take care."

We walk up the short drive to the road, trying to look dignified. We don't look back, knowing that Mrs. Webber is glaring at our backs, seeing us off. Near the parked cars, one of the policemen says, "We could get a warrant and chase them away, but they would just come back."

"What's the use?" I answer, remembering once again that Mrs. Webber's life-style suits her.

Back in our car again, Susan says, "She wiped the floor with us."

"Yes," I agree. "Absolutely."

Suddenly inspired, I suggest, "What if we get her to play bingo with the others down at the Community Service Centre? We could report it as progress."

"I won't be the one to suggest that to her," says Susan.

"Me neither."

We start to laugh and go on laughing until tears come to our eyes.

Simplicity Revisited

Jeanette is still in her night-clothes when I arrive. Her face is drawn. She says, "I couldn't leave him to wash and dress." So I sit in her place on the candlewick spread on the bed two feet away from his.

He sleeps on that bed next to the window. We are in an upper floor flat in one of a number of regimented concrete buildings in Johannesburg's southern suburbs.

Before she left the room, she had said, pressing hard on his shin under the blanket, "Nico, Mrs. Hunter is here." The eyelids on the upper side of his face parted, and there was a dark glitter, no white showing, only that dark gleam from an eye sunk deep in his head, gone when the lids closed again.

I had never imagined I would meet my former client Jeanette again, Jeanette who had walked everywhere in the city dressed like a man and unafraid. Now she is fourteen years older, and her waist has thickened even further. And the Donald I had imagined as her companion in a caravan* next to a rushing stream in the country when I wrote the short story "Simplicity" does not exist.

Her true companion, my present client, Nico, sleeps, and I sit watchful. His breath comes and goes, soft, imperceptible as a baby's breath. Sometimes it seems that it has stopped. His chest does not rise and fall. The metastasized tumours must take up breathing space. His skin is waxy with a sheen like the skin of a baby, and his hair lies close to his skull. Did his mother watch him sleeping so, after he came into the world some seventy years ago?

His face has fallen in upon itself, most of the fleshiness gone and most of the character lines carved by a weather-beaten life ironed out. He is not here; he is halfway to somewhere else,

*caravan: camper trailer

188

dreaming or dreamless in a cloud of morphine, all he needs, plenty, because it does not matter now if he becomes addicted.

The breeze billows one of the open curtains, trapped at its lower end between the wall and his bed, billows like a sail and taps the side of his face. His face registers not the slightest grimace of impatience. That curtain should be fastened more tightly. It should not be allowed to buffet him like that.

*

Nico had roared, taking command of this room, when he had returned from his last visit to the Johannesburg Hospital. He had called for tea, recounted his hospital experiences, hawked and spat into one tissue after another unselfconsciously and with dignity. A great block of a man with a great hard crew-cut head. I pictured him when younger on some rugby team with a thunderous charge and a voice that would carry to television viewers back home.

"No bed at the hospital," he had announced. "Men's problem. Must wait for the operation. They don't want me to smoke."

Soon afterwards, Jeanette told me, "Nico has cancer." She didn't lower her voice. These things happened. "The funeral policy is paid up," she said, "and the gravestone policy."

*

The last time I was here, he sat up in bed and put his legs over the side with his feet to the floor and said, "I don't want you two making plans for me. Listen to me, ladies. I want to die here. At home."

Now he lies here with the breeze around him and the curtain flapping on his face and the towel under his hips hanging over the side of the bed. He has slid down a mountain of pillows, riotous tropical flowers and flourishing cabbage roses on the pillowcases. It is not tidy. The pillows should be plumped up. He should be propped up. But I sit still on the other bed in this narrow room, waiting with him.

Over him on the wall, Jesus in scarlet robe points to his heart of matching colour. On the table between the two beds, a syringe without a needle holds water for dry lips, and a big round wind-up clock ticks obliviously on and on.

The wide window frames steady clouds hanging over a panorama of houses and pylons and towers and mine dumps and the high-rise buildings of a toy city in the distance, all sharp edges softened by a film of dust.

He breathes, and his body, shrunken under the covers, rests. The lapping of the curtain on his face does not tease him back. He is halfway to somewhere else, gone too far to come back.

The Final Years 1990 – 1994

The Alchemist

In the city there is noise and chaos, but the cathedral is a haven of calm. Incense hangs in the air, candles flicker on the side altars, and the red sanctuary light glows. The priest's voice far ahead is a murmur, as if coming from a contented beehive.

A man in a raincoat stands next to me. I didn't notice him when we were sitting side by side. Now I hear the slight rustle of his raincoat, and I steal a glance. He is a small man wearing a raincoat too big for him. If rain fell in here, only his head, the tips of his fingers, and the toes of his shoes would get wet. There's a drought in this part of the country. It's not raining inside, of course, although the ceiling is far above us and I can imagine wisps of clouds swirling up there. Perhaps his raincoat is for protection against the cold of this day.

I steal another glance. He has straight, almost blue-black hair. Perhaps people in his country wear raincoats in winter instead of overcoats. I can't see his face. I want to see his face to be able to read in his features what sort of a man he is.

Why is he distracting me like this? Now he bends forward, and not even his neck is visible. What if he's a flasher? There's the cuff of his trousers just below his raincoat hem, and the raincoat belt clasps his waist firmly. No, I don't think he is a flasher.

While we sit next to each other like this, he makes no claims on me. On my left there's merely an extraordinary stillness, no fidgeting, no small movements. Does he have strict control over himself? Does he sit and meditate for hours without moving when he's not here?

How does his being such a small man affect him? A chip on his shoulder, an arrogance, a need for power, a need to become a hero, to be someone like Nelson, Napoleon, Churchill?

The fabric of his beige raincoat is fine-textured, expensive-looking. He has money and power, obviously. He may be a member of a tong, engaged in opium smuggling, the white slave traffic, or assassinations. I see him at a table with equally inscrutable others, cigar smoke wreathing their heads. They are plotting the next assignment, a new avenue for money laundering, a new method of blowing away victims.

For heaven's sake! I've never been distracted by crying babies, hyperactive children, or a woman in front of me with Parkinson's tremor, but next to this man I cannot get him out of my mind. I'm like someone told not to think of a camel while following an old alchemy recipe to turn dross into gold.

We both stand again, and I notice for the first time his hands resting on the back of the pew in front of us, his surprisingly long and slender fingers. They could be the fingers of a pianist.

No. Now that I think of the raincoat that conceals him, more likely they are the fingers of a safecracker. He is here incognito. He's not here for a religious purpose but for a nefarious one. Yes, being here is his cover. Should I report him to the police?

If only I could see his face, I would know for sure what he is, why he is here. He's driving me crazy.

Ah! The time is nearly here when he—my obsession—must turn to me, look at me, recognize me. This is what I want. When I look into his eyes, I will know who he really is.

He begins to turn to his right, turn toward me. He bends low in a bow of exquisite courtesy. I see his broad, unlined forehead and, below it, short, dark eyelashes over downcast eyes. His hand in mind for a brief moment is as delicate as a moth.

"Peace be with you," he says. I think of the simplicity and serenity of a Japanese garden.

Democracy Was Coming

It was a Friday morning in the summer of 1993 when my colleague Rita phoned. She too was on the committee of the Society for Social Workers. She said she had an invitation to a meeting on welfare policy in Mayfair on Saturday, but she also had an invitation to a friend's game farm for the weekend. So would I go to the meeting or should she phone around the other five committee members?

"Listen," I said, "why are we even considering this? We're so thin on the ground, and we're already trying to decide if we're going to send a representative to the Liaison Forum for Professional Associations as well as to the Health Forum and the Welfare Liaison Forum. We don't have the womanpower to do it all."

This was after Nelson Mandela was released. It was another time when we didn't know what was happening. We only knew that things would change and that things were as bad as they could be already. *The Star* said government departments were disorganized and civil servants knew they were going to lose their jobs and weren't doing any work.

A guy I met who had relatives in government told me some of the top brass had bought homes on the Mediterranean. He didn't have to say they had stolen from government coffers. There wouldn't be any funds left for the new government that we expected would be a black government since blacks were seventy percent of the population.

Some people I spoke to thought the countries that had imposed the sanctions that had ruined our economy would lend us a lot of money to fix it when apartheid ended. I doubted it because loans to countries in Africa to the north of us had no chance of being paid back. Affluent countries wouldn't throw good money after bad in Africa. They were already putting big bucks into countries like the former East Germany, where they might get some return for it.

"This meeting on Saturday is a new initiative," Rita explained. "It's important because it's being hosted by the ANC. We have to explore this avenue, even if some of our members might not like the ANC."

Those members were the ones who couldn't accept the violence instigated by the African National Congress, even though they might agree with its stated aims. I was one of them.

"Is it anything to do with SAHSO?" I asked Rita. "I went to that initiative, and it was an absolute waste of time. Nelson Mandela arrived eventually, hours late as usual. He promised every support, whatever that means, but the speeches at the meeting weren't at all relevant to our work." The first three letters of SAHSO meant South African Health, of course, but I couldn't think what the SO stood for. For some unknown reason, acronyms were proliferating like cosmos on the roadsides; it was hard to keep up with them. We used to call ourselves "the Society," but now we were SSW.

"No," said Rita, "it's entirely separate from SAHSO."

I told her I'd go. After her phone call, I remembered shaking hands with Mandela after the SAHSO meeting and how unexpectedly tall he was and what small hands he had for such a tall man. He seemed to want all the right things for the country, but I wasn't optimistic. The ANC leaders were idealists but had no experience of governing.

I was worried about my own future too. Rumours were going around about social work. The universities weren't going to teach casework—dealing with the needs of particular clients—which I had specialised in. They would teach community work to address the needs of large sections of the population. There would be no government funding of existing welfare programs. There would be completely free health care and free schooling paid for by new high taxes because there were a lot of communists in the ANC. In some ways, things were already changing. Businesses were only donating to politically correct causes. My friend Debbie said the Family Life Centre was going to close, so she was looking for a job in commerce. The trouble was that there would be affirmative action, so she might not be successful since she was white.

Rita's call explains how on Saturday afternoon I came to be reluctantly crossing Harrow Road to get into Abel Road, which would take me south to the city center and then east to the meeting in Mayfair. While I drove I thought about the last committee meeting of our Society for Social Workers. Three representatives from SASWA—the W stood for "White"—came from Pretoria to Johannesburg to persuade us to join them to form one white social workers organisation in the new Liaison Forum, which was to be an umbrella body for professional associations. They gave us a list of their members, and we saw they had mostly Afrikaner names. We told the three that we'd have to consult our members. We were thinking that it didn't seem to us like a politically wise thing to do in view of the coming black government.

After they'd gone, we briefly discussed joining them but didn't reach a decision. If we didn't join, it would look as if we weren't interested in welfare policy. But we weren't optimistic about what the Liaison Forum for Professional Associations could achieve. It seemed to be duplicating at least some functions of the new Health Forum, and in both of the new Forums, Welfare was overshadowed by Health. Also, both Forums had been initiated by the old Department of Health, Welfare and Pensions, now called the Department of Health and Population Development. Even the word Welfare was gone, which did not bode well. The newly named Department was handing administration over to a new outfit called SACOSAF.

I couldn't remember what SACOSAF stood for, but it was another apartheid government initiative, and no one should underestimate the Afrikaners. They hadn't stayed in power for forty years and had it all their own way without being cunning.

We had asked the three social workers from Pretoria if SWASA was still excluding black members. Piet said they had stopped that ten years ago, but they didn't have any black members. We couldn't feel superior, even though we had always been open, because we didn't have any either. They were all in SABSWA, the South African Black Social Workers Association, and they didn't want us to join them. One reason we didn't want to join with SWASA was that joining could alienate SABSWA even more from us, if that was possible. SABSWA said we hadn't been part of the fight for freedom—even though some of us had been—and we weren't going to hang onto their coat-tails now. That shows that the mischief of apartheid wasn't going to stop. Another argument they had against our joining them was that in America black social workers had their own separate association. We couldn't argue with that.

I was driving down beside the Pullinger Kop hill toward Wolmarans Street when I suddenly felt unsafe. Mine would probably be the only white face on this route. I wondered why I hadn't avoided the city center by taking Empire Road and the Queen Elizabeth Bridge. I checked the car. The door button was down, my handbag was on the floor, more out of sight than it would be on the seat, and my window was open only three inches, although it was blazing hot. Those were three of the things the police had said to do to try to be safe.

I had to slow down in crowded Wolmarans Street, where people were crossing the road wherever they liked. The police officer hadn't mentioned the thieves' new trick: the wood-punch that broke a car window quickly and silently. He did stress that if they want your car you shouldn't do anything to risk your life: just let them have the car.

I needn't have worried. People in Wolmarans Street were going about their business, walking and talking and waiting for buses and taxis, and the street vendors were only interested in selling. It was strange how the city center had changed. People from the northern suburbs used to come into town for dinner or to shop at

Stuttafords. Even in Hillbrow, which used to be so cosmopolitan, Exclusive Books and the United Building Society had moved out because it wasn't safe.

After I had left the tall buildings of the city center behind, it was just a matter of following the curving road eastward. The road narrowed into a bottleneck, but traffic was flowing easily and I went with it. A white mini-bus taxi behind me was weaving in and out of lanes. I thought of the taxi wars when rival drivers had shot each other, and a taxi strike had brought everything to a standstill because black employees mainly used those Volkswagen Kombis to get to their jobs in town.

That day of the taxi strike, I worried all day about Pam, another committee member. She had gone into Soweto, and the radio said the situation there was tense. Violence might erupt at any time and our white skins identify us as oppressors.

A lot of other things made us uneasy now. Like the black staff in shops being surly and making us wait to ring up purchases until they finished their conversations with each other. Like hearing that maids had been paying ten rand a month to who-knows-who to own their employer's house when freedom came. Like the shooting of people in the congregation during a service at St. James in Cape Town. Like the "One settler, one bullet" slogan that encouraged murder of every white person.

The mini-bus taxi pulled in behind me. My home was near Louis Botha Avenue, where every day taxis went through red lights and zipped in front of cars with no warning and stopped abruptly to take on passengers.

One day I couldn't get across Louis Botha Avenue for ages. Members of Inkatha, the Zulu political party, were marching to the ANC headquarters in the city center. Thousands of Zulus walked by while I waited at a stop sign. The shops along the way had rolled down their metal shutters and barred their doors, but the tribesmen just walked peacefully, singing and carrying shields and spears, their traditional weapons.

Afterwards, there wasn't even a cool drink can or a wrapper on the ground to show they had passed. Mangosuthu Buthelezi, their chief, was always saying they were disciplined and non-violent, and they proved it on that march. Some of them were shot when they arrived outside the ANC headquarters. The ANC said, "It's nothing to do with us," but who else could have been responsible?

A freeway access point lay ahead. As I approached, the lights changed to amber and I stepped on the brake pedal. At the same time I saw in the rear-view mirror the white mini-bus taxi, crammed full of passengers, coming up fast, much too fast, behind me. I couldn't accelerate and go through the intersection. There wasn't enough time to judge if it was safe, so I let up on the brake and went into neutral, thinking: If he hits me I will not be an immovable object so the damage will be less but only if I am not pushed into the intersection. Dammit! They drive so badly.

Tires screeched, but the mini-bus stopped behind me, not touching my car. I relaxed and waited for red to change to green. Then I saw the mini-bus driver growing larger in my side mirror. I knew it was him, even before I glanced at the rear-view mirror and saw the empty seat in the mini-bus. He bent over close to my window; his eyes in the three-inch gap looking like over-fried eggs, hard and dead, and their whites yellowish with maps of tiny red tributaries. He'd been smoking dagga. (Marijuana was freely available.) His face was swollen, congested with rage; it would have been red if he had white skin. He swayed a little. His raised clenched hands were empty.

He shouted through the opening in the window, "Where you going?"

I wondered why he wanted to know, then thought my mission to the meeting called by the African National Congress might protect me if I told him, but since I couldn't remember the name of the meeting, I just looked at him blankly.

"Why you brake like that?"

"When the lights turn amber, I brake." I hadn't intended to say that, and I recognised I was angry. I remembered the story of the woman who drove off with an attacker's hand pinned in her almost closed car window. Could I do that?

Traffic was moving past us; the lights must have turned green. Uncertainty in his expression told me he was going to return to his taxi blocking traffic in the left lane. He did walk away.

I recalled that I hadn't always braked for amber lights, but I justified it to the taxi-driver as I drove on. You wouldn't have got across the intersection, I said to him, because the light would have been red, I know you have to pick up a lot of fares to make a living, but you shouldn't risk passengers' lives like that. You just do just whatever you like, and the police are scared of you or you give them bribes and they do nothing. It's not right.

I calmed down when small houses and railway lines started rolling by and the white mini-bus taxi was no longer in my rear view mirror.

At the Center in Mayfair there were representatives of many organisations—from SABSWA, SAHSO, CSW; the two universities, RAU and Wits; the Black Sash, and others—as well as delegates from the regional branch of the ANC, which was hosting the meeting, as Rita had said. There was no one from SWASA, the mainly Afrikaner association. And there was no one from the ANC's Welfare Department, which seemed strange since the meeting was supposed to be about the future of welfare and the ANC was going to be the new government.

Carol, who represented CSW, the Council for Social Work, our umbrella body, and was also one of our members, presented a paper on integrating what was happening at grassroots level with the old welfare structure. Then we had to get into small groups to identify problems to be taken up by a steering committee that hadn't been elected yet. Finally, we were to report back to the whole group.

People in my small group spoke about the unmet needs of the blind and the physically or mentally handicapped, whichever group of disadvantaged people they were trying to help. A common theme was that even now there wasn't enough money and they were afraid their clients would be completely overlooked in the new South Africa.

I couldn't concentrate because I kept seeing the taxi-driver's face. When it was my turn, I did speak—although my words sounded stale to me—about the fragmentation of our professional associations, the many Forums dealing separately with welfare issues and proposing different policies, and our urgent need for unity.

During the report back, the black representative from SABSWA complained about the Welfare budget: it looked big, but almost all of it was for pensions, leaving little for community work in the rural areas.

In the end, nobody seemed optimistic. It was decided that the steering committee still to be appointed would be asked to organise a National Welfare Summit to try to put welfare on the agenda for the ANC initiative CODESA, Congress for a Democratic South Africa, for the big negotiations to take place before the first democratic elections next year.

After the meeting, I wanted to believe that something constructive might come out of it and out of all the confusion, disorganisation and lack of readiness for our first democratic government. But each time I tried to be hopeful, the taxi driver's ruined face would rear up in my mind like a portent.

The End of Apartheid

Nelson Mandela had proclaimed, "Force is the only language the imperialists can hear, and no country became free without some sort of violence." Consequently, about 22,000 people, mostly black, died in political violence. Mandela's words that launched the "people's war" inspired my question: was the mob violence and anarchy in South Africa really necessary?

South Africa had been in the process of change since the 1970s. Apartheid had crumbled under pressure from socio-economic factors. Whites comprised only eight million out of a total population of forty million. There was a shortage of white skilled labour, so employers broke the law by employing black people in jobs "reserved" for whites. The law prohibiting strikes by blacks was repealed. Black trade unions were recognised. White private schools and universities admitted blacks. More affluent blacks moved into "white neighbourhoods," and white people acted as nominees to enable blacks to rent property or open businesses in white areas. Segregation gave way on sports fields, parks and beaches, and in cinemas. But the liberation movement ignored the changes and persisted in the belief that apartheid had to be destroyed by force.

The complete collapse of apartheid arrived in February 1990 when President F. W. de Klerk announced that all remaining discriminating legislation would be repealed. He had held discussions with Mandela before his release that month, and these discussions led to the transfer of power taking place without destroying the existing structures of government.

The government proposed the referendum in 1992 on the question of whether all South African adults should have suffrage. Voters, who did not include black people, approved with a sixty-six percent "yes," a vote for true democracy in the country.

I think the violent "people's war" was not essential. The advent of democracy might have taken longer but was inevitable. And with hindsight, a slower handover of power might have been better for the future.

*

I took out temporary South African citizenship to be able to vote in the 1992 referendum. After being sent to stand in one queue after another and waiting in lines again and again at the Johannesburg Home Affairs Department, I saw that time was running out, so I left and raced across town to the black township of Alexandra and its much smaller Home Affairs Department. There I joined a group of Brit ex-patriots in high spirits at the prospect of change. The black official was bewildered both by the number of whites in his office and our cheerful party mood. He allowed us to assist him, to take over really. We pasted our photographs on our new identity forms and made them official by stamping them with the ink-stamp of the Department of Home Affairs that we passed from hand to hand while singing pub songs. That would never have happened at its offices in Johannesburg.

*

Albert Camus, French writer and humanist, believed in the kind of rebellion that he described as finding ways to overthrow a system that do not destroy freedom and liberty or sacrifice the present for the future, ways that support the belief in the sanctity of human life. In contrast, he wrote, revolution rejects incremental change and believes in collective suffering and that the end justifies the means. When I read those words, I felt that he had said something I believed in but could not have put into words.

More simply, Gandhi said, "What difference does it make to the dead, the orphans and the homeless whether the mad destruction is wrought under the name of totalitarianism or the holy name of liberty or democracy?"

*

By pure chance, having been on his way home from a beach near Cape Town, my son John had found himself among the jubilant thousands who waited to welcome the future President Nelson Mandela on his release from long imprisonment. Dressed only in swimming trunks, John was one of the few whites among a multitude of blacks. Other whites were "shaken down" for their wallets and watches, but he had only a towel, and no-one paid him any attention.

John was right: the war he fought in as a conscript was not winnable. In 1990, four years after he left the army, Namibia became a country independent of South Africa.

South Africa itself achieved black majority rule in the form of an elected ANC government in 1994. In April that year, I stood in the sun for hours, moving slowly towards a polling place, together with people of many hues that Anglican Archbishop Desmond Tutu called the "Rainbow People of God," and I voted in South Africa's first democratic election that gave victory to the ANC and Mandela.

After learning the election results, a friend Jim Weinbren and I sat at a table outside a restaurant in Yeoville, Johannesburg, and, putting aside all doubts on that afternoon, we drank a toast to Mandela and believed in the future of South Africa.

Fighting the "Third" Boer War

I can still see Erika as she was on the day in April 1994 when we voted for the "New South Africa." Waiting to cast our ballots, we were standing in a long snaking line on a dusty school playground. The line moved slowly, and the autumn sun beat down out of a cloudless sky. A great number of people had turned out to vote in this first democratic election. We hardly seemed to move in the line, but most people were not impatient: they had waited many years for this day.

Erika, my daughter-in-law, was taller and bigger-boned than I was; her face was broad, her cheek-bones high, her eyes far apart, her teeth even and white, and her straight dark hair shone. She had an enviable capacity for enjoyment, except when things did not go her way, when she would yell dramatically, slam doors and flounce out of the house.

I was staying in Durban with her and Alan and their children before leaving for America. We had always been perfectly polite to each other, but Erika, an Afrikaner, had made it plain that she did not care for America, where everyone was like Roseanne Barr, whom she had seen on television. I told her that was a sit-com, an exaggeration, not realistic.

"But," she said, "characters in Afrikaans television are the way they are in real life. It must be the same in America."

"My mother was American," I reminded her. "And she was not at all like Roseanne Barr on television."

Erika was not persuaded. She implied by silence that one example would not change her mind.

On that day of the first democratic election, it was an uplifting experience to be in line with people of all races. Blue jeans and T-shirts mingled with saris and traditional African dress. Until fairly recently the forty million of us were segregated in different race groups under the Afrikaner Nationalist Party's fifty-year iron rule, but apartheid had crumbled, making this day inevitable, and here at our polling place there was a sense of excitement and optimism.

Erika and I did not share that sense of optimism. We knew each other's views on political parties and had tacitly agreed not to discuss them. I was certain she would vote for the Nationalist Party, as she always had. It didn't stand a chance of getting in, but she would vote her beliefs. Her parents and sister and brother had seen the inevitable future and had emigrated to New Zealand. I would vote for the Democratic Alliance, liberal, multi-racial, progressive, the party of moderation. It would not get in either. Unlike some white people, I could not bring myself to vote for the African National Congress that had inflicted so much violence, much of it against their own people because they belonged to a different political party.

Erika and I often discussed the Second Anglo-Boer War of 1899 to 1902. Erika had heard about it all her life; I had to educate myself by reading. She threw down the gauntlet: "The English invented concentration camps before the Nazis."

She knew that my father was English. Her words conjured up for both of us images of gas chambers, millions exterminated.

"The camps for women and children in the Boer War were really internment camps," I said, "not concentration camps like Auschwitz."

"The English killed hundreds of them. Don't tell me they weren't like the Nazis."

"Erika, sadly, many died, but they weren't killed. They were overcrowded in the camps and malnourished, and they caught every disease going."

As her mother-in-law, I always trod carefully, feeling that I was walking in a minefield.

About this war that was our battleground, Dutch people, who called themselves Boers (or farmers) had first settled in the British Cape Colony. Objecting to the British treating black people as equals, they trekked into the interior, where they established two independent republics, the Transvaal and the Orange Free State. The British managed to annex the Transvaal peacefully, but the Boers did not treat British *uitlanders*, or foreigners, in that territory fairly. When Britain insisted on their fair treatment, the two republics declared war on Britain. Britain was the eventual winner but only after about 26,000 Boer women and children died in the camps Erika and I argued about. It was the death of these children that caused most Afrikaner bitterness.

*

On another occasion, Erika mounted an attack from a different angle (and I thought again of my American mother): "America sent meat for the people in the English concentration camps, and it had barbed wire in it."

"When the hide is removed from a carcass, wouldn't any barbed wire be removed with it?"

"I only know that there was barbed wire in it."

"How can you know that?"

"It's common knowledge."

I clamped down on my tongue. It was said that Afrikaners had long memories, but neither of us had any way of actually knowing the truth. Our arguments mirrored the deliberate separation of British and Afrikaner, descendants of the Boers. The Nationalist apartheid government created separate schools for Afrikaans- and English-speaking children. These children grew up in two different cultures, strangers to the "others," calling each other names, like "rock spiders" and "*sout pens*" ("salt penises)" that alluded to the idea that the Brits had one foot in South Africa and the other across the ocean in Great Britain.

*

Erika opened another discussion: "Emily Hobhouse is my heroine. She got better treatment for the people, and she said those camps *were* concentration camps."

Emily Hobhouse was a British welfare campaigner. "She used that term," I said, "but she didn't mean they were camps for extermination or slave labor. That was fifty years before the Nazi atrocities. It had a different meaning then."

I could see, however, that what I said had no effect on Erika's mind.

I thought but did not say that eight years after the Second Boer war, the two Afrikaner republics became part of the self-governing Union of South Africa, and the descendants of those Boers, the Afrikaners, oppressed the black people under apartheid.

*

Erika struck another blow with: "What right did the British have to take the women and children from their homes, anyway?"

"I think they did it because the women were supplying the Boer commandoes with food and other supplies."

"Well the British troops were being supplied with food, so why shouldn't the Boers have food?"

"I don't know, Erika. I hate war. Bad things happen in wars. Maybe the camps were one of those bad things."

I had grown weary of her attacks and did not know at the time that women and children were moved into the camps for humane reasons after their farms, their homes and crops had been razed.

*

There were things I admired about Erika. She was a good mother, loving, involved, helpful. She was a good housekeeper. She tried to be a good wife to my son.

We got off to a bad start. When I first met her she was half-reclining on Alan's hospital bed after his motor bike accident. She was one of his nurses I was told. Was that proper behaviour for a nurse? And why did she have such an air of owning my first-born, my doctor son? I bristled like Maggie Smith in Downton Abbey.

In Erika's eyes I was unforgivably rude. After their honeymoon, when they set up home, all of her relatives went to visit them. She waited for me to drop in or to call and invite myself. I waited for them to invite me. The relationship of mother- and daughter-in-law is a fertile ground for misunderstanding in the best of circumstances. Different cultures add to that risk.

If anyone was invited to tea, Erika laid out a tea service with a cake platter and silverware on a starched tablecloth. She observed the niceties and, since she expressed an interest in etiquette to me, I gave her Emily Post's book. Years later, Alan told me that she was offended by the gift, thinking I was criticizing her.

On one of my visits to South Africa after I left, Erika said with an air of pride, "In my family, the women have strong voices."

Since I am normally soft-spoken, I took her comment as a put-down but merely said, "Yes, they do," while smugly recalling Erika's previous criticism of Zulu women shouting at each other in conversation.

*

In writing this account, I wondered why I always rose to Erika's baited comments on the Boer War, why I always tried to refute her statements, convinced that I was right and she was biased. Only now can I see clearly that neither of us could know the whole truth of the matter and that the century-old war, safely distant in time, was a way for both of us to harmlessly express our mutual personal antagonism.

Also, both of us, digging in to our positions, had other agendas. I was trying to negate the power of her political party that treated English-speaking citizens with contempt. She, perhaps aware that the time was coming when Afrikaners would become a minority group and a sort of endangered species in what they regarded as their country, was all the more fiercely protective of them.

During my last few years in South Africa, I was on shaky ground, which I would not have admitted to Erika. I voted in the pre-election referendum that black people should be given the vote. I believed that they deserved to govern themselves, but at the same time I believed that they were not ready to do so. We, the colonisers, had kept them largely uneducated and unprepared. Country after country to the north had failed in one way or another. Now that black people did have the vote, I would be leaving the country for others to deal with what followed. I believed there was nothing I could usefully do. Still, I can see my leaving as cowardly. Maybe Nelson Mandela is partly to blame for that feeling I can't forget that he called those of us emigrating "yellow."

Violence increased in the weeks leading up the election. Right wing leader Eugene Terreblanche, who had 70,000 followers, had threatened full-scale civil war if President F. W. de Klerk gave power to Nelson Mandela and the African National Congress. When I booked my plane ticket to leave a month after the first democratic election, I asked the travel agent, "If the airport is on fire then, will I be able to get my money back?" "No," she answered.

Now in 2015, twenty years on, the African National Congress, still in power, is inept and greedily corrupt, and most black people are worse off than they were under apartheid.

On Your Magic Carpet

Begin with the butternut squash at Botha's Hill,
glancing up while peeling and dicing
at the broad sunlit expanse and verdancy
of the Valley of a Thousand Hills.
Chop and sauté onions while a mist descends
and shrouds the thatched-roof huts.
Add the diced butternut and stir
when you begin the descent to the coast.
Coat onions and squash with flour, curry powder
and nutmeg during your second five of the fifty miles
of the annual Comrades' Marathon route.
Take stock, add and simmer. Remember
that downhill is harder on the knees:
just aim to finish. Then smell the sea breezes
and go on to Durban and Eagle Hill Road
above Stainbank Reserve where a boy
is practicing his new flute lesson. Listen
while you sieve or liquidise. Season to taste.
Sit on the back verandah with your family
before the sun goes down, watch
giraffe and zebra stroll below, vervet monkeys
steal the pawpaws while their babies play
on the telephone wires and hahdedah ibis
fly home to roost. When it grows dark, top the soup
with parsley and cream. Now it is the festival
of Divali in Chatsworth, and over there
fireworks light up the ridge. Butternut soup
is good for the heart. Enjoy.

The United States of America
1994 -

Transition

After I returned to the United States in 1994, I lived in Longview, Texas, for three years before moving to Santa Fe, New Mexico.

With the passage of time, I became able to see Ken even more sympathetically. I remembered a friend of his parents, Joan Meintjies, in our sitting room at 5 Saxonwold Drive one evening when I still lived there. They had all lived in Nelspruit in the Eastern Transvaal, but Joan had moved to Johannesburg and visited us from time to time.

On this particular evening, she described a visit to him in a boarding school in Johannesburg, far from home. He could have been in third grade. She found him sitting on his bed alone, his seven-year-old fingers trying to wrap a bandage around his leg, a bandage intended to prevent chafing by the caliper he wore on the leg weakened by polio, a bandage that persisted in unraveling. He continued to battle the ornery bandage, ignoring her offer to help. Both she and Ken seemed proud of the boy's independence. I did not say that even at that young age he might have thought that his feelings were weakness.

But with that memory, at last I could see the lonely boy inside the man, when finally the peace of forgiveness came to me.

About the bullet that nearly killed me, before Ken died he told our daughter Barbara that it was an accident. I know that you don't clean a gun with a bullet in the barrel. I also know that we did not tell each other everything, but if we did say something we always told each other the truth. He and I never spoke about that incident. The mystery remains.

Dragons in East Texas

Not one customer had come into the gift store, and it was now the second day it had been open for business. Jenna peered out through the large window. Beyond the flowering dogwood and clumps of daffodils a small group of picketers stood stolidly on the sidewalk holding posters. A banner stretched limply between two of them.

Jenna had gone out boldly yesterday and asked one of them, "What are you doing?"

"It's a protest." The woman, taken aback by Jenna, had answered with a stony face.

Cars had slowed down, almost to a stop, but had cruised on. Nancy commented to Jenna, "Customers must be too intimidated by the protest to come in."

Jenna phoned the police. "I'm sorry, ma'am; they are on public property. We can't do anything."

"It's a criminal mischief, if anything is," she fumed, aware as she said the term that she was not sure of its meaning.

"They are not causing a disturbance."

"They are disturbing me." He had remained polite, but unmoved.

"It's only a gesture," Nancy consoled herself and Jenna. "They'll get bored and go away."

Jenna took hope from the words. She would not have gone into this venture without Nancy to lean on: Nancy's earth-mother appearance made her seem solid, a source of strength in this new and alien world, so different from the South Africa she had recently left. She answered, "After all the money we've put into this, they'd better go away."

They had polished the already sparkling glass counters and showcases and had swept the already dust-free corners; they had straightened the greeting cards and gift wrap; they had rearranged the scented candles, the puzzles, the handmade vests and afghans, and the ornaments; they had glanced at the mobiles, immobilized without a breeze from the door to set them in motion. And they had looked out of the large front window from time to time. Uniformly dressed in jeans and long sweat-shirts, the picketers were amorphous, faceless enemies from the back. They kept vigil in shifts; as the day wore on their shirts changed slightly, but their numbers remained the same.

Today—at opening time—their forms were back on the sidewalk, and the morning sun slanting on the banner outlined the letters on it backwards: TI-CATAC. Reversed, the letters spelled out CATAC-IT and made as much sense as the other way.

"Why have we been hiding from them?" Nancy erupted. "Letting ourselves be intimidated. Let's go and talk to them." It was unusual for her to get so heated, Jenna thought, the strain is getting to her.

"What have we got to lose?"

The men and women standing side by side remained still and impassive and looked through the two women approaching them on the Odum Road sidewalk.

"Hi! I'm Jenna." She craned her neck to look up at the baby-faced man who had been with the group yesterday and seemed to be the leader. "Howdy, ma'am, I'm Dwain."

"Why are you doing this?"

He frowned and said nothing. He must think it's obvious, Jenna realized, and she tried again. "What is CATAC-IT?"

"Citizens Against The Anti-Christ, ma'am. In Texas."

"The Anti-Christ!" Her head reeled. "How do you figure that?"

"That sign there." He gestured to the painted board attached over the door of the store: blue letters on white, chosen to complement the frame house painted blue and trimmed with white.

She read the words on the board aloud, as if seeing them for the first time and trying to see them as he would: "Mystical Things."

"Yes, ma'am."

It made no sense. She remembered the afternoon on the porch when she and Nancy brain-stormed names and discarded dozens. Too ordinary. Too copy-cat. No pizzazz. Mystical Things was from a song. They had hummed the gentle, haunting tune, remembering only one line of the lyrics: "Down, down, down where the iguana play."

"Mystical Things?" she repeated, but on a rising note. "What's wrong with that?"

"Mystical," he said, puzzlement on his face. "You know what it means."

This isn't real, she thought, I'm in a nightmare. "What does it mean?"

She could see he thought she was acting dumb. He turned to the woman beside him. Her poster read, "Keep East Texas Safe For Our Children." She nodded, and her nod seemed to say: they would play dumb; that's their strategy; just state the truth.

"It means the occult," he answered and turned his pure sky-blue eyes on her.

"The occult, my foot! Where are you coming from? Go away and leave us alone."

Nancy stepped in. "Dwain, please understand. We didn't mean the occult when we thought of the name. It just means something that's not everyday and ordinary, something special and a little bit magical."

"Magical," he repeated, and he glanced at the woman beside him.

"And not black magic, either. Listen, if we changed the name, would you stop doing this?"

"I don't think so, ma'am."

"There are only gifts inside," Jenna appealed. "It's only a gift store." The faces of the other picketers were as obdurate as Dwain's.

There seemed to be nothing more to say. Jenna pulled Nancy's sleeve. "Let's go."

Inside, Nancy said, "They think we're trafficking with the devil."

"So now we are witches. That's nice. What if we invited them in? They could see it's just a gift store."

"If they did come in, maybe they wouldn't like the Buddha."

"What? Oh that. Who knows?"

Jenna thought about the pewter Buddha she had selected, not in ivory, that was too expensive and not politically correct nowadays, and not the one with a smile like the Mona Lisa and a bare tummy you could stroke for good luck, but the Laughing Buddha, standing legs apart in his loincloth and holding a ball in each hand high above his head and laughing. Full of joy. She had thought the world must seem different when your god can enjoy a good belly laugh. So different from the Man of Sorrows.

"I'll put it away just in case."

"Open from 8 to 6," a small sign on the door said, and they stayed in the showroom until six, then they prepared and ate supper, which Jenna did not taste. She went to bed early, but slept only fitfully; her mind was hollow and dark, and thoughts scuttled in its corners. In the morning Nancy said, "Let's try again."

Nancy greeted the group: "Good morning. We have an idea. Won't y'all come in and have a look round? We want to show you it's only a gift store, like any gift store."

Dwain answered, "No thank you, ma'am. It wouldn't do any good."

"Why not?"

He looked away and shuffled his feet before replying, "We know you've got a dragon in there."

For a crazy moment Jenna thought he meant a real dragon and he was afraid; then she remembered the pewter dragon, a lovely thing, a companion piece to the Laughing Buddha. "What's wrong with that?"

"Look here." He pulled a sort of miniature computer out of his pocket and poked at the keys. "I've got the whole Bible in this. Just a minute. Revelation twelve three. Here."

She went round under his shoulder to peer at the tiny screen as he read, "'A second sign appeared in the sky. A huge dragon with seven heads and ten horns.' See.

"'Its tail swept a third of the stars from the sky.' See. 'The dragon stopped in front of the woman so it could eat the child as soon as it was born.' And see here. 'War broke out in heaven, and Michael with his angels attacked the dragon.' And now. 'The great dragon, the primeval serpent, known as the devil of Satan, who had led the world astray, was hurled down to the earth and his angels were hurled down with him.' It's plain as day, isn't it?"

"Yes," Jenna answered helplessly, "but the dragon we have isn't like that."

"I'll tell you something," he volunteered, "I wouldn't have a thing like a dragon in my house. Not that it can do anything itself, you know, but it's an opening. You could be letting Satan in."

"But evil only comes in if you want it to, if you let it."

"I'll tell you something else. My son will never play Dungeons and Dragons. Children have killed after playing it." His conviction was rock hard. Any argument she could raise would be feeble against it.

Inside the house, they slumped. Jenna groaned. "What are we going to do?"

Straightening up, Nancy said, "We have to get back to our jobs next week, and I'll tell you something else. We're stuck with all this stock, and after payments on the loan there isn't going to be much to live on."

Jenna calculated: the loan plus the mortgage subtracted from their salaries, and they would have to be vegetarians, never mind no restaurants, no movies, no . . .

"And another thing," Nancy went on, "you should phone your father right away and tell him it's off. There's no use having him mooning around here with nothing to do."

They sighed, almost in unison, and Jenna knew Nancy, too, was thinking of his disappointment. "You're right. At least he has some friends in Vermont, people to spend time with. But darn it! He was so excited about managing the store. He hasn't been so alive since Mum died. What shall I tell him?"

"Say the opening has been delayed. Technical reasons."

Jenna was on the phone for a long time. "So?" questioned Nancy.

Jenna laughed. "Oh, boy. My ears must be more used to the Texan drawl than I think. He could have left England yesterday: not even a hint of his years in Africa."

"What did he say?"

"Well, he got it out of me—about the protesters, I mean—and he did his 'When I was in Poonah' thing. He said (and she made her voice gruff and plummy), 'What balderdash! When I was in Northern Rhodesia, the natives ran away from chameleons. They wouldn't come near my house when I had a soapstone chameleon in the lounge. Had to put it away to get the place cleaned.' The worst of it is he wants to come down more than ever. Said he's looking forward to a good fight."

"That's all we need." Nancy rolled her eyes up to the ceiling and remained looking upward briefly before she asked, "What do you know about dragons?"

"Well, we know it's not a real animal. It's legendary, and in paintings and drawings it looks like an alligator, but with a scaly body and wings and feet like a lion's."

Nancy mused, "When I was a kid, I had a story book about a friendly red dragon. And we used to sing, 'Puff the Magic Dragon lives by the sea.'"

"One thing is for sure. A dragon is different things to different people. Like Dwain. What does it say in your *Dictionary of Symbols*?"

Nancy went off and came back with the book. "It says, 'The dragon is a fabulous animal and a universal symbolic figure found in the majority of the cultures of the world.' There's more. It's an amalgam of elements from various animals that are particularly aggressive and dangerous. And this looks important: the Sumerians thought of it as 'the adversary, a concept which later came to be attached to the devil.' Seems that Dwaine is right. Should we be scared?"

"Scared?" Jenna repeated. Her face brightened. "Let's go to the library and find out more. I'll put the 'Closed' sign up. We won't be losing any customers, and maybe the dragon-fearers will think they've won and go away."

"No, you go. I'm sorry. I have a splitting headache from all this. You go, and I'll try to have a nap. I'll have supper ready when you get back."

*

Jenna returned when the sun was going down; her eyes were gleaming and her cheeks flushed. "I've got pages and pages of notes. I'll just skim through and pick out the exciting bits. This is a gold mine. Back in the 25th century BC—maybe before—people worshipped a female god, who had different names. Sometimes it was a female creator, like, listen to this, Isis, the Goddess from whom all Becoming Arose, Ashtar, Queen of Heaven, and Queen Nana the Creatress. This was in the Near and Middle East thousands of years before Abraham. It says, and I'll read this, 'Man's part in conception was not realized, so the female was revered as the giver of life. She was seen as the only parent and producer of the next generation.' Did you know that?"

Nancy looked mystified. "No, I didn't, but what has that got to do with dragons?"

"I'll get to it. Then what happened was, after those thousands of years of people worshipping the goddess, invaders came down from the north in about the third century BC. They had a male god, called Marduk, who was sometimes a father god, but also a young warrior or storm god, who tried to destroy the older female god. He's supposed to have murdered his great-great-great-grandmother, the creator goddess, to take over her place and become King of the Universe. She was called Tiamat then. And now listen to this. Myths that came from those times portrayed the female god as a serpent or dragon, usually associated with darkness and evil, in a battle with the storm god."

Nancy threw herself back in her chair, raising her hands in a gesture of surrender. "Wait a minute. You're going too fast for me. Is that saying the serpent or dragon represents the female god?"

"Yes, and they represent the whole belief system the people had about the goddess that the people from the north were trying to wipe out."

"Okay, I've got it now. What else?"

"The book says this myth appears as the conquest of the serpent Leviathan by the Hebrew God Yahweh, and it may survive in the legends of St. George and the dragon and St. Patrick and the snakes."

Nancy interrupted, "They told us in the convent St. Patrick drove snakes out of Ireland, and that's the reason there are no snakes there. But, really, he got rid of goddess worship?"

"Uh huh. It seems so. It took a while, but eventually the goddess religion was suppressed by the Hebrews and by the Christians in the first centuries after Christ, and it was nearly forgotten."

"Nearly forgotten! I never knew it in the first place."

"Right," Jenna went on, "and when God was thought of as a woman, women had high status or equal status to men, but when men gained superiority, that history was suppressed."

"Wow!" breathed Nancy. "Have we eaten of the tree of knowledge or what? Now I'm remembering things. Pictures of those clay figures—women with big boobs and bellies—in that Ancient History class I took. They told us it was just a cult. And all the time it wasn't just a cult? It was the religion everyone had, that everyone believed in?"

"Yes, it seems so."

"Well, I'll be darned. It's enough to turn you into a militant feminist."

A comfortable silence settled upon them.

Jenna broke it. "We have found the dragon and it is us." They laughed.

They continued with their own thoughts until Jenna commented, "I don't think Dwain would be interested in hearing our news, do you?"

"No," Nancy agreed, "it's odd how some people have no humility about their beliefs and yet we want to protect them."

"Isn't it? And now I know what we are going to do. We'll start by getting rid of that dragon over there. I'll hide it like Dad hid his chameleon. Then we'll have the sign repainted. Tomorrow. Is 'Gifts for You' bland enough? We'll see if they can protest that?"

"Don't forget, Jenna, we'll have to go downtown and apply for a change of business name. And you can phone your dad again."

"No problem." Jenna began to sing, "Down, down, down," and Nancy chimed in with, "where the iguana play."

On Caddo Lake

We leave the village named Uncertain
and now our motor boat sets out on Caddo Lake,
its cargo's just my grown-up two with mates
and lunch and me, the matriarch who's full
of urgent, selfish hope for all of us
to get along so well the younger pair
will not pursue their plan to travel on
to find another place to settle down.

We thread our way through lilies, giant-sized,
the buds flamingo-like with graceful necks
that open into saucers, cream and white,
and seem to breathe as lotus used to do,
inducing trance.
A broad expanse reveals itself; a searing sun
infuses everything; the vast unmoving lake
is edged at its far rim by bent-kneed cypress trees
in shrouds of Spanish moss. The haze is bright,
so luminous it hurts my eyes.

As we cruise slowly on there is no breeze
and we are pressed between the weight
of air and silver shining glare of water.
We sit inert and crushed. The boat glides on
and landmarks vanish. We'll be lost I'm sure
or in some uncanny way diminished. I think again
if they should leave I would be quite bereft.

We stop and start in weedy shoals of green
and ages pass until it opens out
and then we see a line, an orphan string
hung from a tree, and at the end of it

we find a turtle knotted in the twine and desperate.
We cut it loose, it swims, and we, afraid,
begin to joke about the ways that Texans have
of shooting first and asking questions afterwards,
and going on we sing some songs of home,
like *Nkosi Sekelel' iAfrica** and Sarie Marais.**
In soft and mournful cadences we sing
but with defiance too of feeling alien.
We say this place has never heard these words,
nostalgic tunes, and wouldn't understand.

The sky and sun look down impassively;
the dark unmoving water holds its peace.
When we glide on, the land ahead reveals
a channel that we take for change of scene and mood.
Before a bend we spot a bird and stop.
A hell's angel on water-bike bears down on us
to miss by inches, speeding by wide-eyed with fright.
We breathe again, but switch the motor off.

The great blue heron stalks—majestic—
and with backward-seeming forward gait goes
about his life. From thrones and powers come
he's close as one can get to mystery.
He moves beyond our sight, so we chug on
and out on open water we decide to stop for lunch.

Our faces, arms, are red. In dappled shade,
reflected sun, we loop a rope around
a cypress root. With little appetite
for food, my two begin a water-fight,
through playful splashes acting out a piece
of adult sibling rivalry. They stop and stare,
like us, at bread and chicken scraps that lie
untouched where cast upon the water.

No life exists in these dark depths to take a bait.
Is this the domain of an underworld
and does some Charon ferry souls below
across a river like the Styx?

Again I doubt that we can find the way
we came, and yet I have a mind to know
and understand this weird primeval place.
As in a dream we venture farther. Water,
air and sky are luminous; the world is shimmering
and in this haze all elements are one.
We seem this time, as if in answer to my hope,
about to merge, united as a family.

Putt-putting on, we find a spit of land
and beach the boat. There's certitude in feet
on solid earth and walking. Three of us
return and take the boat into a creek,
a sort of bayou, where a submerged line
gets snagged against the hull, and loosing it
we find a catfish hooked. "A coward's way
to fish," says one. "Let's set the creature free."
It's done, but when we join the others back on land
an argument begins. "It's someone's livelihood."
and "Why did you let the turtle go?"
and "Can't you see the difference?" and more
and more. No way to know who's right or wrong.
I only know the day's in shreds, my wish denied.
A dull foreboding numbs.

Just then the sun is darkened by great wings.
We see our heron lift himself against the air
with slow and steady strokes, oblivious of us.
For me it seems to bring a sign of grace.
We find our way and starting point, of course.
We separate. The family disperses.

Once more I learn that wish and will
are not enough to alter things like this
but like a kind of consolation prize
the great blue heron stays with me
to be an icon in the coming days.

* *Nkosi Sekelel' iAfrika*: Lord Bless Africa, in Xhosa by Enoch Sontonga, 1897

** Sarie Marais: the name of a young woman in an Afrikaans sad love song.

In the Dark

I wish I hadn't accepted when Gregory, my landlady's son, invited me to this party. He's been to Algeria and Morocco, countries at the other end of the continent from South Africa, where I've come from, but he thinks we have something in common. I hate parties, hate introducing myself to strangers and trying to start a conversation. I'll wait a while before I do my party duty. It's lovely out here on this large deck attached to Gregory's house with the desert all around and the beautiful *Sangre de Cristos*, Blood of Christ Mountains, on the horizon. I lean against the railing of the deck and watch other guests talking animatedly, flowing easily from one small group to another, clusters of young people fluidly dissolving and reforming. I had hoped to meet people who might become friends but should have known Gregory's friends would all be young, much younger than I am. I sip from my glass and pretend to be at ease while the sun sinks and horizontal rays light up the scrubby juniper and piñon trees scattered on the pale terracotta landscape. Across the arroyo, a yurt stands out, a white shape set down on the tawny soil, strangely out of place so far from its Himalayan home. As dark descends, people begin moving down the steps and across to a shallow pit ringed by round stones. A log fire burns in the pit. I join the other guests and sit with them on the ground around the fire. I'll be less obviously alone here, and the warmth of the fire will be welcome when the evening grows colder. The fire lights up the concentric rings of faces, but doesn't penetrate the dark beyond. I can imagine a vast unexplored territory surrounding us.

A didgeridoo just outside the circle of light begins a bass-voiced dirge. It conjures up the Australian outback, not so different from this high desert in New Mexico. Fingers slap bongo drums, rhythms find each other and settle into a common harmony. The rattling of seeds in a gourd—a maraca—joins in, and the didgeridoo falls silent. The faces of the guests in the firelight are rapt.

Despite sitting so close to other party-goers, I still feel cut off from them. Perhaps this is the way it will always be in Santa Fe, this place of faux adobe, prayer flags and Hindu chanting, of a carved wooden St. Francis keeping company with a concrete Buddha, of sacred geometry, crystals and smudging, of Our Lady of Guadalupe, of candles in paper bags, Free Tibet bumper stickers and that yurt across the way. Can I find a home in such a smorgasbord of beliefs and cultures?

Of course I can settle here. Those are just external things. What do they matter? I need to stop making comparisons with the familiar people and places and ways in South Africa, the comfort of the known, the good things that I miss. I have to make a fresh beginning.

But before I can go forward lightly into a new life, I must get rid of the burden of other memories I carry. I think I need to talk it all out and for someone to understand what my life had become there. I need someone to hear about the shots and police sirens in the night, security gates in the doorways of homes, banks, restaurants, burglar bars on windows, razor wire on garden walls, handbag searches at the malls, my telephone calls tapped, looking under my car for limpet mines every morning, and the fear of an impending civil war.

I had started to try to tell Gregory's mother Norma about the bad memories, but I could see she could not even begin to visualize them. She interrupted, saying, "I think you have post-traumatic stress disorder." She reminded me of the man who had asked me to tell him about witch doctors. I told him what I knew, and he turned on his heel and walked off without a word. When I got over being astonished and hurt, I thought he must have wanted to keep his romantic view of Africa. He couldn't bear hearing that in Kwa-Zulu, where my son Alan was the superintendent of Nkonjeni Hospital, babies had been given enemas of battery acid "to make them strong" and had been brought to the "white man's hospital" only when they were dying in agony.

Now, there's a new sound of drumming: *djebe* drums, African drums, approaching. It's like an echo of the nearby drumming, and in the distance people are shouting indistinct words. The faraway drumming grows louder, the voices more raucous. The guests sit in silence, waiting. Are they afraid? Their eyes shine, their faces pallid as mist.

A procession bursts out of the night with wild cries, dark skins, colorful African tunics and matching cotton fezzes in a blur of red and yellow. The drumming grows insistent. Are we being attacked? A large man with the build of a chief leaps onto the rim of the fire pit and dances unsteadily, weaving and swaying on the narrow ledge between the feet of guests and the boundary stones around the fire.

The chief sings, "Everybody take a body. Everybody take a body."

What could he possibly mean? He's sweating in the cool air. The whites of his eyes are blood-shot in the firelight. Is he drunk? Been smoking pot? His five followers trail after him, dancing around the fire. Their drumming so close is much too loud, but the party guests look entranced. They don't believe we are being attacked. Why doesn't Gregory introduce the newcomers?

Their bodies pass between me and the scarlet flames licking the air, and I see again the television footage—that played over and over back in Johannesburg—of a fire in a township, a body drenched in petrol burning on the ground, a gleeful crowd dancing around the agonized victim. I remember Winnie Mandela brandishing a matchbox as a symbol for freedom fighters, encouraging more of those killings: murders of their brothers because they joined a different political party. I want to stand up and run and keep running until I reach the mountains at the horizon, those mountains named for their red hues, for the blood of a savior, but I can't move. Maybe Norma was right; maybe I do have PTSD, but it's been three years since I left South Africa: I should have recovered.

The chief is repeatedly singing a line in a foreign language that could be Swahili. He calls out at the top of his lungs, "C'mon, everybody. I can't hear you." He wants us to sing with him. What horror might my mouth commit if I sing words I don't know? Words that might be the slogan of the Pan African Congress: "One settler, one bullet." Words that might be an incitement to rape?

"More firewood," the chief commands. "We want to see your faces."

The fire flares up; the faces around the fire are serene, almost worshipful. I am not one of them, separated by my memories. Despite the warmth of the fire, I shiver. I still can't move, can't get away. The invaders could be chanting some version of "*Uhuru, Amandla,* Black Power." I am back in the old grip of fear of a civil war in which blacks would outnumber whites many times over, more than thirty million against eight million.

I draw my knees up to my chest, then realize I am trying to make myself smaller, invisible. Stop it! The dancers must be a visiting troupe, that's all. They probably performed at the Lensic, and Gregory met them after the show and invited them to this party.

Someone touches my arm, startling me. It's only Gregory. He looks concerned. Algeria and Morocco, where he spent time, are not like South Africa, but he should understand. I need his understanding to rescue me. I reach for his shoulder, draw him toward me, and say in his ear above the din of the drums and voices, "Darkest Africa."

Darkest Africa: shorthand for the dark continent, for the *Heart of Darkness*, for exploiter and exploited, for the ravages of colonialism, for fear of a native uprising.

Time is suspended while Gregory's face remains blank. The words "Darkest Africa" hang in the air between us.

Finally he speaks. With a puzzled frown, he asks, "Dark is taffeta?"

A Good Deed

Gail had never wholeheartedly regretted adopting the four kids until the day she waited for her name to be called in the holding cell for women below the Alabama Criminal Court. In the cell, the flickering of the harsh fluorescent lights had suggested that justice was uncertain. How had she landed in this predicament?

The other women were laughing and joking among themselves.

"Hey, honey!" one of them called to her. "What you doing in here?"

"My son told them I assaulted him and showed them his bruises."

"How old your boy?"

"Just turned seventeen."

The women, full of curiosity, crowded around her.

"He seventeen, and you just a itty-bitty thing."

"My son, he know I gonna kill him if he put me in jail for whopping him."

"I beat mine all the time, jus' don' leave no bruises." They all laughed.

She was not as street-wise as her companions charged with other crimes. They included her in their camaraderie and, most likely, would start serving time that day. When her name was called, she stumbled up the stairs to the court, wrists in handcuffs, legs almost failing her.

"You are charged with assaulting a family member."

When asked how she pleaded, she answered, "Not guilty."

"Bail is set at $10,000."

Pleading was a formality. She *had* hit Shaun. He had stolen from her and lied once too often. When he returned home, she had hit him with the plastic vacuum crevice tool she had been using to clean the spaces between cushions on the couch.

"Shaun, my iPad and Kindle have disappeared from my bedroom. You're the only one who's been in the house since I left this morning. Just for once, tell me the truth. Did you take them?"

"No, Mom, I didn't." Looking her straight in the eye, he lied.

He would sell them for a fraction of their cost or give them away to any girl who caught his eye, as he must have done with all the other things. She lost control then and struck him again and again on the thigh. He was bigger than she was, but she was the parent in his eyes, so he did not strike back, although he raised his hand as a warning.

"You're not allowed to beat me. Stop!"

She did stop then, hauled back to her senses. He glared at her with narrowed eyes, hatred in them.

"I'll kill you. You better believe it," he said in a level voice. She believed him.

He bruised easily and showed his bruises to the staff at school the next day. Shaun was the most obstinate child they had ever had to deal with, but they were obliged by law to report his accusations. Regretfully, they notified the child protective services, and their representative removed him from the school to a place of safety.

That same day another caseworker went to Shaun's sister's school with a police officer and took eighteen-year-old Nancy, a slow student, to another place of safety. Two days later, she was returned to Gail and William.

Nancy told Gail, "I wouldn't lie to them."

"About what?"

"I wouldn't sign a paper that said you whacked me."

"You were a brave girl."

"I'm never going back to that school. I thought the police were taking me to jail. I didn't know what I did wrong for the police to take me away."

Nancy remained unwilling to return to school, shamed in the eyes of her classmates and afraid of the police coming for her again. Gail agreed to find another way for her to get her GED.

On the Internet, Gail researched murders of adoptive parents by adopted children. A high proportion of these children killed their parents. No actual figures for murdered parents were available, not like the sixteen percent of serial killers who had been raised by adoptive parents.

It was chilling to find out that there seemed to be no sympathy out there for the murdered adoptive parents. It was assumed that those parents got what they deserved because they must have abused the children. On the other hand, there *was* sympathy for the children who killed. It was assumed that killing their parents was not their fault. The children's circumstances caused them to suffer from "radical attachment disorder" and justified their killing.

Taking Shaun's threat, "I'll kill you," seriously and unable to forget his hate-filled face, she put the family home on the market. As soon as it sold, she planned to buy another house, and its whereabouts would remain undisclosed.

She learned from the child protective services that Shaun would not be returned to her and that he had not recanted his threat. She remained watchful at home and at work, always on guard against his appearance with a gun, every day a living nightmare. She was walking underwater, dragging herself through life from morning to bedtime. At night she lay awake, trying not to think,

Weeks later, she finally faced the reality of the court case: she had been charged with a felony. If convicted she would not only be jailed, possibly for a year, but would lose her license to practice as a Doctor of Oriental Medicine. It was incredible. All her life she had been law-abiding with not so much as a parking ticket.

She advertised for a business partner, and when Dr. Burns applied, she told him in confidence about the pending case. "It wouldn't be good for the practice if the patients think I abuse my children."

"Of course."

"I need someone to help keep the practice running, to treat the patients on those days I don't have the energy to deal with them. And if the worse comes to the worst, I'll need you to take over the practice, buy me out."

The contract was drawn up and signed. A prison term was the worst she could imagine; that morning in the holding cell had been bad enough. If it came to that, she hoped proceeds from the sale of the practice would help her start over afterward in some other career, whatever it might be. She could not think so far ahead.

What could she have done differently? Twelve years ago she had decided not to have expensive medical procedures in the hopes of bearing a child. There were already too many children in the world yearning for a home with loving parents. When the four siblings became available for adoption, it was clear that her vocation in life was to give them a home where they could have a good life and be together.

The trial period with the children in their home was difficult, but that was to be expected after all the foster homes. The kids would settle down when they were secure, when they knew they were wanted and had a permanent home.

Other couples were willing to adopt a maximum of two siblings, and the authorities were grateful to let all four go to a good home. Gail basked in the glow of the world's approval and even, briefly, felt heroic.

The six of them stood up in the informal Children's Court, and each child in turn, Evelyn, Leroy, Nancy and Shaun, aged ten, eight, six and four, heard the friendly lady ask, "Do you want William and Gail Silverton to be your new parents forever?"

"Yes," each one said.

"Do you agree that in the future your last name will be Silverton?"

"Yes."

Everyone in the courthouse smiled, happy for the new family.

Gail had learned that the four had been removed from their original home because of neglect and suspected abuse, after which they were separated and moved from one foster home to another, and that some of the foster homes were abusive.

After the adoption, both girls exhibited precocious sexual behavior. Nancy, the younger one, screamed every day for hours on end. Gail realized that Nancy was expressing feelings she could not speak about; she tolerated the screaming and tried to comfort the girl. William could not stand it and would slam out of the house. Nancy screamed herself out and became calm and docile, although never completely in contact with reality.

Shaun, the youngest, was impossible to control from the start and did not change. He was expelled from the two pre-schools she enrolled him in, and after he entered elementary school she was called for a parent conference almost every day. Nothing she or the teachers could do, no punishment, no deprivation of privileges or treats or toys, nothing would induce him to do anything he did not want to do. But love and patience would eventually do their work.

Within months of the adoption, William had said, "I can't do this anymore. I only said I would adopt because you couldn't have children and it was what you wanted."

"But you went to the parenting classes with me. You signed the papers."

"I know, but it wasn't what I wanted. I want my own children."

"Well, you'd better go then. I can't undo the adoption."

She couldn't expect him to be moved by how damaging his leaving would be for them. She kept the house, which was something, but he paid little toward the children's support because she earned more than he did. She received money from the state for the children's medical expenses but not for the private schools where they could receive the individual attention they needed to help them catch up. She hired home help to supervise them and to drive them to after-school activities when she could not leave the practice. She would have to try to earn more.

*

Twelve years after the adoption, at the time Gail was charged with assault, the two older children, Evelyn and Leroy, had grown up and gone out into the world. They had refused the free higher education the state provided. They did the least they could, working at burger joints, getting fired when they did not turn up for work, and couch surfing. It was disappointing, but Gail hoped that with more maturity they might realize that they could improve their lives by working hard and might even find it fulfilling to give something to the world.

She had looked forward to seeing the court ordered counselor soon after she was released with bail set. He seemed cold and vaguely accusatory, not at all what she had hoped for. When she learned that he was employed by the child protective services, she understood that he was not impartial and that was why he always seemed to assume she was lying. She attended the required number of sessions with him but was careful about what she said. An innocent remark could be used against her.

To retain an attorney, she withdrew $5,000 as the first installment from investments earmarked for her retirement. It would be money down the drain if she were convicted, but at least he provided a sympathetic ear for her worries about the case. He was eccentric with a handlebar mustache and old-style Southern manners. He addressed her as Dr. Singleton and told her he wished to be called Mr. Keller, which was fine with her as long as what he promised came true.

"Don't worry," he said.

"I can't not worry."

"It will go away. Just wait and see."

How could a court case go away? He notified her when court dates for hearings were scheduled and of his applications for continuances. Months dragged on while her nights remained sleepless and she forced herself to eat. She lost weight, dropping from a hundred and thirty pounds to a hundred and ten and went on losing. She was exhausted.

After Shaun's threat to kill her, her belief in the children had begun to crumble.

Shaun's former teachers, Sally and Betty Lou, who were also her closest friends, had been the only ones to tell her beforehand, "We think you're crazy to think of adopting four kids."

Now she understood, "I never thought I'd say this," she told them, "but I'm wondering if I should have adopted them."

"I'm sorry, Gail," Betty Lou said.

"I couldn't have loved them more if they were my own, and I've given them everything I thought they needed, but maybe I couldn't make enough of a difference in their lives."

Sally had an inspiration: if the court knew what she and Betty Lou knew, she told Gail, the case would be dropped. They drew up affidavits about Shaun's behavior at school and what they had seen of her parenting and submitted the witnessed and notarized affidavits to the court. They infected her with their optimism.

"The truth shall set you free," said Sally and laughed.

Mr. Keller called Gail. "Dr. Silverton, the teachers' affidavits have not been accepted. The caseworkers succeeded in keeping their evidence out of the hearing."

Gail, Sally and Betty Lou went to lunch together. Gail mostly listened, drowning in disappointment and weariness.

"Those caseworkers can be eighteen-year-olds with hardly any training."

"I heard they get paid for removing children."

"Not exactly paid. I heard that to keep their jobs they have to remove a certain number."

"All four of them have attachment disorder, Gail. It's more extreme with Shaun. He's a sociopath, what they used to call a psychopath."

*

It has been a year since she was charged. She has taken a taxi to the courthouse. Sally and Betty Lou have arranged for time away from their school and are waiting with her in the corridor outside the courtroom for her case to be called. She tries not to think of what the outcome might be. Worrying will not help. Why is Mr. Keller late? Is that the reason the case has not yet been called? What will happen if he does not arrive?

"The State of Alabama versus Silverton!"

With her friends she enters the courtroom, then walks alone and uncertainly towards the front. She is directed to stand on the other side of the railing facing the judge. She sees the familiar face of Mr. Keller. He looks back at her steadily. Be calm, his look says. Everyone in the courtroom is silent. All activity seems arrested. She is numb. Behind the judge, the stars and stripes, hanging limply, promise liberty and justice for all. Too much to hope for. She has packed the personal items she might be permitted to have in prison.

The bailiff enters the room, shrugs and says to the judge, "Witnesses for the prosecution are not on the premises."

"Case dismissed," says the judge. "The defendant is free to go." He stands.

"All rise," calls the bailiff.

While she stands, the realization that the caseworkers have not turned up takes shape slowly in Gail's mind. Previously, Mr. Keller had told her there was a high attrition rate of employees in their system: thirty to seventy percent. He must have relied on that when he asked for continuances.

Mr. Keller approaches her. He shakes her hand and says, "Congratulations. And your felony charge will be erased from the record."

Sally and Betty Lou come forward with open arms and hug her. "Let's go out to dinner to celebrate." She agrees to meet them later. Although she is too dazed to feel like celebrating, she needs to thank them for standing by her. While her friends are still smiling, full of delight for her, she begins to believe that her ordeal is over, that she really is free to walk through the outer door of the courthouse, the way she came in.

All at once, she understands everything. It is only by chance that she is free, only by chance that justice has been done. It has all been an enormous mistake. Partly her mistake. She could never have made up for what had been taken from the four siblings. It was also the child protective services' mistake. They should not have removed them from their birth mother. They should have done whatever it took, given whatever assistance was necessary, to make it possible for the children to stay with her. Or they should have allowed the children to stay with a responsible relative nearby, where they could have everyday contact with her, their real mother, the woman who deserved them.

Altar of Air

The ordinary day
and clear morning sky
are demolished.

Aviation fuel flares,
concrete and glass dislodge,
steel girders melt.
The invincible spine
of the city is shaken.

Far above us
heat shrivels your skins,
your lungs gasp.

But facing that inferno, some of you
choose to sacrifice yourselves
on the altar of air

on the way to the river of lamentation
and beyond that
to the eternity of the waters of Styx.

I'm holding you now with my tortured breaths.
Take hands for courage.
Ahead is a great leap, a sacrament
to transcend the horrors.

Hold fast for these short airborne moments.
while you spiral down the wind
and thundering in your ears are wings
to carry you aloft.

The Orange Dress

Returning to her desk in the study, Anna opened the invitation—hand-made on hemp paper—to Robert's second wedding. At last! He and Laura already had a child, a toddler. Robert was a little old to have fathered a child. What was he thinking?

It couldn't be helped. Now that they were to be married, the important question was: what to wear to the wedding? It simply could not be a little something off-the-shoulder with bra straps displayed. The young had such bad taste. She sent an email to Laura asking about the color scheme for her bridesmaids. Laura replied at once, "Don't worry about it, Anna. Just wear whatever you want."

Silly woman. If she knew what she wanted, she wouldn't have asked. Maybe she could Google bridal wear or look through one of those thick expensive magazines at her hairdresser's salon. It had been quite a while since she had been part of the entourage at a family wedding.

Turning to the screen, she read back and forth emails between her other son and her daughter, with copies to herself. Tim wrote, "Helen is being her usual bitchy self." Helen announced, "I am not going to Robert's wedding if Tim will be there." Tim came back with, "I will not be emotionally blackmailed." Tim's wife chimed in, "Helen is being unreasonable."

Anna's hands rose unbidden from the keyboard as if wanting to knock their heads together. Well, they would sort themselves out, and one or other of them would be available to drive her to the airport and accompany her through the dreadful security they had these days. Last time, the TSA took her aside into a little room and wanded her for a second time. How could she possibly be a terrorist? If they tried that again, she'd insist on having her lawyer present.

That night Anna woke with a start and realized that she had forgotten to Google bridal wear. Whatever she decided to wear, it must do herself justice as the mother of the groom and not be too obviously trying to upstage the mother of the bride. She had not worn high heels for a while, but just this once would not do her toes too much damage. As for the dress, it couldn't be white or black, obviously, or short, which would lack a certain gravitas. Nor could it be a pastel color. No one with any dress sense wore pastels these days.

Unable to sleep, she went to the study. Opening Facebook, she saw that Tim and Helen had unfriended each other, and Tim's wife had written, "Because of the unpleasantness, Tim and I won't be going to the wedding, so Helen can go instead." Helen posted, "Before Tim changed his tiny mind, Donna and I had made other arrangements. Sorry, Robert." Whereupon, Tim's wife wrote, "Helen should cancel her other arrangements. What can be more important than a family wedding?"

Anna said aloud in the night air, "Remember: you pledged not to give unwanted advice to your adult children." If neither Tim nor Helen decided to go, she'd inquire about an airline escort, like the ones they had for children traveling alone. To avoid the temptation of sounding off on email or Facebook, she pondered her unresolved question. Suddenly she knew. She would wear the long slinky dress with slits right up her thighs. It had been hanging in her closet since the day she bought it; she'd never had an occasion to show it off. It was in shades of orange with a tracery of leaves and delicate tendrils, a hint of green, just a touch. That should knock everyone's eyes out. Enough of always sitting in the back seat wearing beige.

Robert emailed the family, "Since so many people are not coming, Laura and I have decided to cut down on expenses and have a less formal wedding. We plan on going to the courthouse in the morning and having a celebratory lunch with just a few guests in the park down the road."

Well, the orange dress with high heels might be a little overdressed for a picnic in a park but would have to do. What about green highlights? Maybe not. The burning question now was: what color nail polish would go with orange? Not red or pink, for sure. And not black: she wouldn't want to look witchy, at least not in a Halloween sort of way. Orange nail polish might be overdoing it. She should be able to find nail polish in an agreeable shade of apricot to go with orange. If necessary, she would take the dress along to the store to find a good match.

Satisfied, she went back to bed. When she woke, the first thing she did was to take the dress out of the closet and over to the window to see the leafy design in the light of day. It was not the long dress she remembered but a short sleeveless dress with matching jacket. Never mind. The jacket would be perfect for the courthouse and could be removed in the park for a more al fresco appearance. And it was silk with a lovely soft, flowing, cool feel. It would be a knock-out, actually, with green nail polish. She would be ready when the day arrived and would be seen if not heard, rather like being a child again.

At the computer with coffee, she read bride-to-be Laura's new email: "Robert and I have talked it over again. Because Anna is the only relative coming, we can't see the point of having a public ceremony. We'll just exchange vows and then tell everyone that we're married. It will be a valid common law marriage, anyway. In Colorado all you have to do is live together for three years."

The only relative? She swallowed hard. Well, a common law marriage was better than none. The young would live their own lives, and she must move with the times. Very slowly, Anna took the dress from the back of the chair where it lay, enclosed it in its protective plastic bag, and hung it in its place in the closet. An opportunity to wear it might still arrive. Helen had recently "outed" herself and Donna. The laws were changing, changing as ponderously as a steamroller but just as surely.

Thank You

My thanks go to friends in writing groups who have improved my words and encouraged me along the way—Susan McDevitt, Lonnie Howard, Enid Howarth, Jim Roghair, Ursula Moeller, Joe Mayer. Further thanks to Connie Josefs for inspiring me during her leadership of Osher Institute writing courses. And final thanks to John Daniel and to my sister Julie Matthias for their editing of the last drafts of the manuscript (any errors remaining sneaked in afterwards).